CHICKEN SOUP
FOR THE
BEACH LOVER'S
SOUL

Memories Made Beside a Bonfire, on the Boardwalk, and with Family and Friends

Jack Canfield
Mark Victor Hansen
Patty Aubery
Peter Vegso

Backlist, LLC, a unit of
Chicken Soup for the Soul Publishing, LLC
Cos Cob, CT
www.chickensoup.com

Chicken Soup for the Beach Lover's Soul
Memories Made Beside a Bonfire, on the Boardwalk, and with Family and Friends
Jack Canfield, Mark Victor Hansen, Patty Aubery, Peter Vegso

Published by Backlist, LLC,
a unit of Chicken Soup for the Soul Publishing, LLC. www.chickensoup.com

Front cover design by Andrea Perrine Brower
Originally published in 2007 by Health Communications, Inc.

Back cover and spine redesign by Pneuma Books, LLC

Distributed to the booktrade by Simon & Schuster. SAN: 200-2442

Publisher's Cataloging-in-Publication Data
(Prepared by The Donohue Group)

Chicken soup for the beach lover's soul : memories made beside a bonfire, on the boardwalk, and with family and friends / [compiled by] Jack Canfield ... [et al.].

p. : ill. ; cm.

Originally published: Deerfield Beach, FL : Health Communications, c2007.
ISBN: 978-1-62361-059-3

1. Vacations--Anecdotes. 2. Beaches--Anecdotes. 3. Beaches--Recreational use--Anecdotes. 4. Anecdotes. I. Canfield, Jack, 1944-

GV191.6 .C45 2012
796.5/3   2012944769

PRINTED IN THE UNITED STATES OF AMERICA
on acid free paper

28 27 26 25 24 23 22 21   04 05 06 07 08 09 10

This book is dedicated
to those who find tranquility,
healing, and love at the beach.

Contents

3. LETTING GO

4. TRANQUILITY

5. SPECIAL MEMORIES

6. INSIGHTS AND LESSONS

Introduction

What makes a child beg to run barefoot in the damp sand and build castles with moats, only to see their creations dissolve at day's end? It's the same feeling that tugs at an elder's heart to walk quiet distances on a chilly day by the shore. A beach lover's soul is etched in the sand, no matter what region of the continent. They flock yearly to the warm sunshine by the coast, pave trail ways in the snowy sand with their cross-country skis around the Great Lakes, or use the "slowed-down" pace of fall in which autumn leaves are caught at a nearby stream.

This magical place, the beach, casts a spell on us that loosens the tightest grip of anxiousness on a human while refreshing the weariest of souls. Even the most cantankerous of us all find peace within a hard exterior. We walk, rest, and watch our children sift through the sand to find every seashell or sand specimen, then listen to them shriek in delight when another gem is found. Perhaps they are teaching us to find beauty in every bit of sand dollar—so that we can shed life's daily despairs and discover the importance of acknowledging our greatest human assets while accepting our biggest challenges with grace and wisdom.

Our beach-loving readers prove many times, if not

thousands of times, that all that sparkles is not necessarily gold, but may be a spot of sand that overlooks the deep ocean or a crispy-cold lake dancing with rays of the sun's ever-present optimism. The stories told in this book range from the quite funny to the deeply soul searching; they all share the same thread of how the mystique of the sand and water directed people to experience a new attitude or outlook. The sands of life do not betray their visitor's dreams or worries; they pack as many secrets as granules on a beach and continue to answer our hearts with a wisdom that only time and nature understand.

CALIFORNIA

San Diego, Pacific Beach

California Surfing

Malibu Pier

CALIFORNIA

San Diego, Pacific Beach

Crystal Pier

Oceanside, California

Sunset at California Beach

CALIFORNIA

Francis Beach, Half Moon Bay

Half Moon Bay State Beach, California

Bixby Bridge, Big Sur, California

CALIFORNIA

Francis Beach, Half Moon Bay

Cliff over Half Moon Bay, California

1

UNDER THE BOARDWALK:
ON LOVE AND LEARNING TO LOVE, COMPANIONSHIP, AND FRIENDSHIP

Tell me thy company and I will tell thee what thou art.

Cervantes

Sand Prints

They walked along the shore,
arm in arm, hands entwined.
Pressed in warm, wet sand,
their footprints left behind.

It was their special time together,
on the beach at the end of the day.
Enjoying the beautiful sunset,
watching young children play.

Their heads are close together
as they plan their life ahead,
his arm goes around her shoulder
as they decide it's now time to wed.

She raises her face upward,
as if to receive a kiss,
a look of joy in her eyes,
as she dreams of wedded bliss.

He pulls her very close to him,
promising to keep her from harm,

to provide a safe haven for her,
where she'd be loved, safe, and warm.

They walk off into that beautiful sunset,
arm in arm, their hands entwined,
as the tide creeps upon the shore,
erasing all those footprints left behind.

Tomorrow they will again return,
their path to trace once more,
leaving more footprints behind
on that sun-drenched gulf shore.

Pamela Gayle Smith

Connections

It's all emotion. But there's nothing wrong with emotion. When we are in love, we are not rational; we are emotional. When we are on vacation, we are not rational; we are emotional.

Frank Luntz

"Look up, over there," David said, with a seriousness in his voice that caught my attention.

"Where? What?" I asked, diverting my gaze from the sand at my feet, where I combed for seashells.

He pointed toward the water, a whole ocean of water, endlessly rolling toward the shore in dense waves.

"Watch there," he said, pointing to a specific spot.

Nothing looked out of the ordinary to me. "What am I looking for? Did you see something?"

David shook his head. "But wait," he said, reaching for my hand.

And so I stood there on that Carolina beach, next to my friend, my beloved husband of twenty-five years, holding his hand, waiting, watching with him in anticipation of something very special.

When do a man and woman really fall in love? During a first dance, a first kiss, the first time they share souls? When they make up after their first fight? After their hundredth fight? Each morning when they wake up, side by side, to the promise of a new day? Or is it when they tumble into bed at night, exhausted but content from the responsibilities and accomplishments of supporting and raising a family? Maybe when an illness or brush with death has taught them that life is a sacred gift and so very fleeting? Or perhaps it's each and every time their hearts make a connection. . . .

The roar of the ocean filled our ears, the salty spray of the water caressed our faces, and the wind rustled our hair as our eyes scoured the water. Then, just to our right, coming into the line of our peripheral vision, something crested briefly at the top of a wave and then dipped into the recess. Moments later, it crested again. A dolphin! No, two dolphins! The pair swam side by side, riding the waves and paralleling the beach.

We laughed out loud, giddy like children. Only once before, years ago at Virginia Beach, had we seen dolphins swimming in their natural habitat. What a treat this sighting was! I turned to David. "Had you seen them coming?"

"No," David said with a sheepish grin.

"Then how'd you know they'd be there?"

He shrugged his shoulders. "Something just told me to look up."

I gazed at my husband. This wasn't the first time something inexplicable (a whispering heart or intuition, perhaps) had made us look up or away, or take one path and not another. I've learned not to question some things in life, but rather offer thanks on their behalf, as now: the gift of standing on the beach in the afternoon sunshine, holding my husband's hand, and watching the dolphins. I don't know if they were lifelong mates, as David and I, but in that instant, they were together, just the two of them, journeying through their life in the water, as were David and I, on the land. . . .

I fell in love with David the first time we slow-danced, our tenth-grade year, and again a year later when we shared a warm kiss after walking together on a cold winter's eve. I fell in love with him the first time I watched his eyes crinkle when he laughed, and even more deeply when he was not ashamed to let me see him cry. We rarely argue anymore, but I swear I fall in love with him all over again whenever we kiss and make up. Where could a woman find more love for a man who has awakened each morning of his married life, and, without a single complaint, provided a living for his family? Seven years ago, when I thought I saw him take his last breath during a serious illness, I never loved him so much as I stood in the hospital corridor and pleaded with God not to take him from me just yet. But today, I fell in love with him all over again as our hearts made another connection, another memory. . . .

David and I continued our walk along the beach. We watched the dolphins journey up the coastline, bobbing in and out of the waves, until we could see them no longer.

Was it random that David had taken the day off from work? That we'd decided to run away to the seaside for a few hours while our children were in school, and it just happened that, as we walked along the beach, two dolphins swam northward? I think not. I believe the universe conspires to give us gifts, both large and small, to confirm that we are on the right path and that all is as it should be. Our job is simply to remain available and aware—and stay open to the connections.

Tracey Sherman

Be Like the Ocean

Sometimes, a walk on the beach can change your life. And sometimes, it can happen far from home, on a foreign shore. Disappointed with love, a young woman left her native Switzerland and arrived in England, hoping to learn English and to forget. I left my native Massachusetts, wanting to know more about the land of my grandfather, hoping perhaps, to remember. We both settled in a small English seaside town with a view of the ocean (with one's neck stretched out the window). Walking along the lonely sea one evening, we met, and eventually we fell in love. We spent several weeks together until I returned to New England, unsure what would become of this tender romance, but sure of my deep feelings for this stranger on the shore.

Hoping to decide what to do, I rented a small seaside cottage in the winter on Cape Cod. I spent long walks on the deserted beaches, taking in the sights, sounds, and smells of the ocean, while on the other side of the Atlantic, a Swiss girl in England did the same. One day, as I strolled a lonely shore, I was approached by an elderly woman who spoke with a foreign accent and was about to change my life. I told her about the young woman I had met and about my uncertainty over what to do and was intrigued with her story: she had emigrated from Italy after the war and had faced a number of hardships, including the language, the cultural adjustment, and homesickness. Through it all, she knew it was right, because of one thing: the love of a man, a young American she had met in Europe. As our conversation ended, she grabbed my arm, reached down for a seashell, and said: "Be like the ocean, Arthur. It always knows what it is called to do in life without anyone telling it. We can too if we can remember something." She paused, looked away for a second, then turned back to me and whispered as softly as the rushing waves, "Listen to your heart," and she pressed the seashell into my hand.

I followed her advice. Today, I live in Switzerland, a country without a beach. But my wife and I spend time each year on the shores of Cape Cod or England, where we walk together, holding hands, many years later. Often, I turn my collar to the stiff Atlantic breeze, place my hand in the jacket pocket, and find a twenty-five-year-old seashell. Be like the ocean.

Arthur Bowler

EDITOR'S NOTE: *The woman on the beach changed my life. After several months of staying in touch mostly by writing letters, I heeded the woman's advice. I listened to my heart and traveled to Switzerland to be with the Swiss girl I had met on the English shore. My wife and I have been together ever since.*

A Love Affair Never Forgotten

When our four children were young, we took our first vacation to Daytona Beach, Florida. I remember how in awe of the scenery I was when we entered Florida, the beautiful Sunshine State. It was much different than we were accustomed to in our homeland state of Illinois.

The palm trees stood tall and regal, and the tropical flowers among the lush greenery made me think we had arrived in a location much akin to paradise.

Arriving in Daytona, I savored my first-ever glimpse of a beach; I fell in love with the ocean rolling in from somewhere out in the deep.

As our week provided unrelenting pleasures, I came to love scanning the sand along the water's edge for seashells, small sea critters, and other possessions brought in and deposited as treasures at my feet.

I waded out into the water, up to my shoulders, and scanned the water's floor with my feet, looking for assets transported from other lands by the turning of the tides.

Our children sat daily in the sand, constructing castles and forts, only to watch the waves carry off their fantasies to lands where only God, visionaries, and fairy-tale dreams could foretell what lay beyond the present.

Like a greased baby bottom, we stayed covered and protected from the rays of the sun. Yet my husband, whose feet had been confined for years beneath dark dress coverings, was shocked at the introduction of the sun intensified by the sand as he walked along the beach. Soon his feet took on the appearance and painful distress of trapped lobsters.

I had not known the power water possessed, beyond what came through copper piping back home in Illinois. I stood mesmerized as waves in their might rolled over themselves, again and again carrying me with them into the future where dreams lay and memories are collected.

Our children stood, leery of the ocean's imposing authority, fearful of the bashing abuse, petrified of yielding, but determined to step out to conquer the strength of its deep currents. They soon overcame, triumphant over the insults inflicted upon them; they took their stance and tasted the salty rewards.

At night we walked the abandoned beaches, looking out at the moon reflecting off the blackness and listening to the tide bringing in more treasures—what would dawn reveal buried beneath a footstep? What creatures would we find trapped behind, gasping, searching for a lost love—the depths of the sea?

Soon our vacation came to an end, our days swallowed up in seven rolling tides. Seven days of paradise blissfully came to an end, carried away and stored as future treasures, memories never to be forgotten.

That vacation has been many years ago and our children are all grown; their children are now learning the beauty and might contained within great bodies of water. They are finding pleasures untold and seeking treasures of their own. They are forming their own love affair with beaches and casting upon the waters their own dreams and visions. They are storing away albums of memories, visual pictures for lifelong memories.

My husband and I have gone on to walk other seashores, and form other love affairs with beaches around the world, but like one's first love affair, we have never forgotten our first: Daytona Beach.

Betty King

My Two Loves

"Gonna be another hot one today," I complained to my husband.

"Yeah, those Santa Ana winds are really blowin'."

I hated these "devil winds," as they are called by local Southern Californians. They made people cranky and forest fires rage, not to mention drying out my skin and hair, and making me an irritable mess. I also feel cheated. Just when I should be pulling my sweaters out of mothballs and watching the trees change into their fall dresses, here I am dealing with hot, dry, itchy weather.

"Maybe tonight we can head down to the pier," my husband, Paul, yelled as he ran out the door to work.

"Ah, relief will come," I said to no one in particular, although the dog did lift his head off the floor long enough to sigh. I had forgotten the one perk of this season: going to the beach in autumn. That was always our one salvation from the oppressive heat of the dry desert winds.

As promised, Paul made it home on time, and after a light dinner, we drove the four miles to the ocean.

For some reason, the beach never failed to thrill and entice me. You'd think since I was raised a Southern California beach girl, I would be used to its charms by now. But no, the ocean at night, the waves crashing on the shore, the moon glistening off its surface, always seemed magical and mysterious.

And so, on this balmy fall evening, Paul and I linked arms and joined the mass of humanity looking for a spot on the pier to cool off. We passed families fishing together, lovers embracing, the single person staring out to sea, and couples laughing, just out for a stroll. One thing was certain—in their own way they were all enjoying the ocean's gifts, such as the cool breeze, the salty spray, and an inner calm beyond description.

Below us, surfers rode the waves, children tried to outrace the foaming tide, and others dug for either clams or buried treasure. Who knew?

"It's too crowded up here," Paul called over the gull's cries and the squeals of the children. "Let's go down on the sand."

"Okay," I replied.

As we descended the steps to the sandy bottom, thoughts flashed through my brain. I remembered years long past when Paul and I cuddled around a beach fire-pit, lingering kisses on a beach blanket while the waves lapped the shore, and how we gazed into each other's eyes over the fire.

"Hey, a penny for your thoughts. You look a hundred miles away," Paul asked.

"Oh, I just realized how much the beach has played a part in our love life."

"Well, let's not stop now," Paul said, taking me in his arms.

As we kissed I shut my eyes and felt the breeze caress my shoulders, the hot "devil winds" long forgotten. I knew right then I was in the arms of my two loves—my husband and the beach.

Sallie A. Rodman

Did You Turn on the Water?

"Did you turn on the water?" he asked.

"Yep, it's on," I answered. "Can't you hear it?"

"Hmmm, maybe. Let's see."

We sat up, peered over the headboard, and separated the blinds to gaze at the shallow waves softly lapping at the shore. We smiled. And so our day began.

We were newlyweds living in a house on the sands of Pensacola Beach. It was a dreamy place to begin married life—even if it was only forty-five degrees outside. The Florida panhandle's weather was more like lower Alabama than Florida, and only the hardy or young-and-broke couples braved the storms, the chill, the lack of insulation, and small space-heaters to live "romantically" on the beach during the winter. In spring, people flocked to the white-sugar sand and clear blue and turquoise water, but until then we had it to ourselves.

It was the beginning of a life near the water. Although we had not been raised near the sea, my husband's career as a navy pilot led us to ports in Corpus Christi, San Diego, even the Sea of Japan. We discovered strength as a couple from the ocean, the constant waves, the changing moods of the sea.

The joys of beachcombing, long walks in the ebbing surf, finding shell treasures as they wash up to shore, picnics on the sand, and watching the sun disappear below the horizon fill us with quiet peace and pleasure.

In times of crisis, we also long for the beach, where we ponder its majesty and power, reminded that we are only like small grains of sand as we watch the waves spilling onto shore and continuing on and on. The wonder of God's power calms and soothes us, enabling us to deal with whatever crisis life deals us.

When our young daughter fell from and was trampled by a horse, we sat in the hospital at midnight during her emergency surgery. Frightened, we struggled to focus on happy times, including memories of sun-swept days at the beach as our little girls frolicked in the surf. Within a few months, we were able to renew those moments; they romped in the breaking waves while we searched for seashells.

When my father-in-law suffered a stroke, we walked miles on the beach as we grappled with how to best care for him. Later, bringing him to the boardwalk to look at the expanse of ocean and shore gave him a sense of contentment for a time. My husband commented, "You can be a beach lover without getting sand between your toes."

Last year, for our forty-fifth anniversary, our children gave us a night at the most luxurious beach hotel in Southern California. Upon waking the next morning I heard that familiar question:

"Did you turn on the water?"

"I think so. Let's go look."

And hand in hand we went through the French doors to the balcony, where the Pacific Ocean lay before us, waves lapping at the shore, and we once again were filled with that familiar hope. We smiled.

Jean Stewart

Mr. Crescenti's Beach

Age does not make us childish, as some say; it finds us true children.

Johann Wolfgang von Goethe

I was born and raised in New York City. My parents met, married, and moved into a large apartment building with a view of the East River. Dad had been a lifeguard at majestic Jones Beach on Long Island during his teenage years. Mother had developed a love of the beach as her parents owned a summer home directly by the Atlantic Ocean. They decided to pass this mutual passion on to their only daughter. Thus, at an early age, I was taught to swim and enjoy the feeling of sand between my toes.

When I was seven years of age my parents bought a small summer cottage on the eastern end of Long Island. We began to spend the summer here, embracing the joy of being beach aficionados. I loved these times and had many adventures walking the beach, swimming in the surf, digging in the sand, and just watching the waves hit the shore.

Each year, the day after Labor Day, the car was packed and we would begin our journey home to the city. Riding

back I would write down all the memorable events of the
summer and save them to read at future dates.

Once we were home, school beckoned, my friends surrounded me, and life became the norm of daily routine.

But the beach was still part of me. I slept under a blanket adorned with the prints of colorful shells. All the summer photos were taped to my bedroom wall. The seashells
that I had collected were displayed on my dresser. Cold
weather surrounded me, but the memories of the beach
kept me warm.

The years passed quickly, and I married and became the
proud mother of two wonderful daughters. We lived five
blocks from my parents on the same city street. I taught at
the neighborhood school that I had attended as a child.
My mother said that I went into teaching so that I could
spend the summer at the beach. And we all did—together,
as a family, in the same beach cottage that I knew as a
child. Dad had added two bedrooms and a large family
room to the once-small residence so that we could all
enjoy the beach together. He also loved inviting the
neighbors to visit as much and as often as possible. I never
remember a time when the house wasn't bursting at the
seams with people. Laughter filled the air, and food
passed hands in all directions.

My daughters loved that so many of their friends could
visit with them during the summer. At night the adults
would sit on the beach and swap stories, enjoying the
smell of the salt air and the gentle breeze off the ocean.
The children always found something to do, usually end-
ing with a marshmallow roast before bedtime.

My youngest daughter, Donna, always loved to cuddle
on my lap at night and listen to the adults' stories. She listened intently, resting her head on my shoulder, entwin-
ing her long fingers within mine. I loved these times, so
simple, yet so memorable.

They say that history repeats itself, and so the day after Labor Day the girls were packed into the car and headed back to the city. Their summer snapshots were stuck to their bedroom wall and their seashells placed on the dresser. The school bell rang, and summer was over.

Each day the girls and I would visit my parents after school. Mom would set milk and cookies on the table, and the girls would swap stories until my father left for work. They would then walk my parents' dog before we left for our apartment. Invariably they would return from the walk with goodies from one of the neighbors. They knew all fifty families that lived in the building, and were always doing errands for one family or another.

Donna, who was now eight years of age, had a standing order to deliver a loaf of Italian bread to an older couple that lived on the same floor as my parents. Mr. and Mrs. Crescenti lived in a very small one-bedroom apartment at the back of the building. They had emigrated from Italy after their only daughter died at the tender age of five. Mr. Crescenti had always been my favorite neighbor during my childhood. A short stocky man, he lived life with a smile on his face and a twinkle in his eye—and had the longest mustache that I had ever seen on a man. When he laughed the ends moved up and down.

I would bring the morning paper to the couple before I went to school. I always received a homemade cookie for my effort, which I devoured on my walk to school. I liked to visit with the couple and hear their stories about the "old country." Their apartment was filled with photos of their daughter, Angelina. She was a bright-eyed youngster with dark curls, a sweet smile, and chubby cheeks. Sadly, she died after coming down with a high fever of no apparent origin. The Crescentis' small seaside village provided no doctor, and by the time one did arrive from the city, it was too late. Mrs. Crescenti went into a deep depression from which she really never recovered. Mr. Crescenti dealt with the loss by moving them to the United States. He was a shoemaker by trade, and he opened a small store on the street below my apartment building. I called him "Boom-Boom" when I was a child and it stuck. He did not talk about his daughter during my childhood, but appeared to have no problem discussing her with my daughter Donna.

Donna had taken over my job, delivering the couple's loaf of daily bread. Mrs. Crescenti had become an invalid and never left the apartment. Mr. Crescenti sold the store and spent his days caring for his wife, keeping their small apartment spotless, and cooking—always cooking. As you exited the elevator the wonderful aroma of some simmering dish would fill your nostrils. The apartment door was always open, and one could hear Mr. Crescenti singing in Italian as he prepared dinner. Donna would deliver their bread and then walk the family dog with her sister, Tracey.

One afternoon she did not return from the Crescentis', and I guessed that a batch of cookies had lured her away. After an hour it was time for us to start for home so I knocked on the Crescentis' open door.

"Come-a in," Mr. Crescenti shouted. I found the three of them in the living room. Donna was perched on Mrs. Crescenti's lap gazing at an old leather-bound photo album. She stroked Donna's hair as she pointed out the pictures to her. "This was my Angelina when she was two-a years old—she look just-a like you, Donna." I held my breath. It was the first time I had seen Mrs. Crescenti smile in years. I let Donna stay with the Crescentis' that night. She slept on their sofa and spent the weekend listening to all the stories about Angelina. Donna continued her visits for about a year, until Mrs. Crescenti passed away peacefully in her sleep.

That summer my parents invited Mr. Crescenti to stay

with us at the beach. He was elated. He spent hours walking the beach, telling the girls stories about his village in Italy. His childhood fascinated my Donna; she couldn't get enough of his stories. He played in the sand with her, helped her build sand castles, and walked the beach with her constantly. They walked hand in hand, digging their toes in the sand, watching the gulls overhead, and laughing—always laughing. Staying with us that summer allowed him to embrace his grief and find some peace for the future. He returned to the city and started to work part-time for the young man who had bought his store. All went well for a few years, and then Mr. Crescenti suffered a stroke. We were all devastated. He had no family, other then a few cousins back in Italy, and my parents became his caregivers. The residents of the building assisted as much as possible, and Donna continued her bread run for the dear man. She would slice the bread and put it alongside the dinner plate that my mother had prepared for him each night. Donna would stay and tell him about her day at school while he ate. He always asked that she tell him a beach story before she left for home.

That summer, as we left for the beach, Donna appeared sad. She knew that Mr. Crescenti would be well cared for by all the neighbors during the family vacation. Still, Donna called him each night and described how the beach looked and how the sand felt between her toes. Her devotion brought tears to my eyes.

One afternoon we watched as she dragged a large plastic bin from the garage to the beach. She would sift sand each day with an old kitchen colander. She collected what she called "special seashells" and put them in a lined shoe box. We never asked what she was doing; we knew she was on a mission by the look on her face.

The bin returned to the city with us that year. We helped her carry it into Mr. Crescenti's apartment. We lifted the old man's feet into the sand. Donna arranged all the shells on the sand and got out our summer photographs. We all sat on the sofa as she told him all about her summer. "Dig your toes into the sand, Mr. Crescenti," she said. "It's the same sand that I walked in all summer long." He smiled and did as she asked, while a tear ran down his face. She showed him each shell, and he listened with great joy. Donna did this for the next six months, every day, seven days a week. She missed her playtime, movies, birthday parties, and many other events. It didn't appear to matter to her. Each day she would pull out the bin, now called "Mr. Crescenti's beach," and place his feet in the sand. They would talk and laugh for hours together.

Mr. Crescenti passed away, as did his wife, in his sleep. His ashes were sent back to Italy for internment with his beloved wife and daughter.

Donna appeared lost, a part of her life gone. Mom and Dad, along with many of the neighbors, assisted in cleaning out his apartment. Donna retrieved the bin of sand and brought it into my parents' living room. Here it stood for nearly a week. At the dinner table one night she announced that she had a plan, and we all smiled.

That Sunday a memorial service was held in the lobby of my parents' apartment building. Donna delivered a written invitation to each neighbor and requested that all who come bring a jar with them. All fifty families were represented that morning. Donna had pasted all the photos from the old leather-bound photo album on poster board, and they stood in the lobby for all to see. My father and I read a verse from a book of poems about the sea. Cookies from the bakery where the couple purchased their daily bread were delivered to the lobby and enjoyed by all.

My father introduced Donna and lifted her up on a small table. Slowly she read a letter that she had written the night before:

Mr. and Mrs. Crescenti lived in this building for a long time. They watched my mom grow up. They were very friendly. Mrs. Crescenti made the best cookies in the world. Mr. Crescenti was a great shoemaker. I love the beach, and he did too. I brought his beach here today because I know it would make him smile. I think he would like his beach to stay here with all his friends. Please, can you take some sand home in the jar that you brought with you and keep it to remember Mr. Crescenti?

Not a dry eye could be seen in that lobby.

Each neighbor scooped up some sand and took a little part of Mr. Crescenti's beach home with them that day.

I stood in awe, watching the event, feeling my heart swell with pride at the little girl who had made this all possible.

As I write I stare at her picture and a little bottle of sand that for me is a message for all times: Life is like sand on a beach. It can blow away if you aren't careful.

Yet, like love, it can never truly be destroyed.

Anne Carter

Life's a Beach . . . and Then You Drive

The surf's up and it's finally time to hit the beach! For months, I had pored over so many *Coastal Living* magazines that I'd practically given myself sunstroke in anticipation.

I had waded through pages of sun-filled layouts with families happily walking together along the sand. Smiling Coppertone kids beamed over buckets full of perfectly formed seashells and posed in front of Biltmore-sized sand castles that they'd constructed, I imagine, sans parental participation. Moms and dads looked blissfully relaxed in lounge chairs, while their carefree children frolicked in the ocean without a jellyfish or icky floating thing in sight.

Unfortunately, you won't find many photos like that in our family album. Faster than you can say "Vamos a la playa," it's clear that a day at the beach with my brood isn't exactly, well, "a day at the beach."

After an hour of overpacking the car with a stack of rusty sand chairs, a leaky cooler, countless sand toys, and as many boogie boards and skim boards as Ron Jon's Surf Shop carries, we look more like the Beverly Hillbillies than the well-heeled beachcombers I'd seen in those glossy periodicals.

The kid's backseat bickering begins before we even make it down the driveway. It continues as we lug our gear across a Sahara-wide strip of sole-searing sand. We wince in pain as we try to sidestep the shrapnel of broken shells along the way. The schlep seems endless as we ritually wander and stop—at least three times—until we're sure that we've found just the right spot.

It's only after we've fully unloaded and arranged our chairs in perfect alignment with the sun that we realize that the tide is actually coming in. My husband does not look amused as we frantically chase scattered flip-flops that have been swept away by a small tsunami, and we move yet again—back to where we stopped in the first place.

After fighting gusts of gale force winds, we take a moment to bask in the glory of getting our rickety umbrella planted upright and thankfully without impaling any neighboring sunbathers. Then comes a heated Greco-Roman wrestling match to get the children covered with their sunscreen, which by their protests you'd think was really acid.

My husband, with a solar-induced migraine, quickly tires of a minefield-like game I call "Which bikini-clad body on the beach most closely resembles mine?" Then we begin the losing battle of trying to keep track of all our pails, shovels, and stolen hotel towels—most of which are already half buried.

It's only a matter of time before the kids begin a chorus of complaints about the sand in their eyes and the grit between their teeth or somewhere else in their swimsuits. I wonder if I hold a seashell to my ear, would I hear the sound of a child whining?

But eventually we settle in and find our rhythm with the ebb and flow of the sea. The boys excitedly start digging their way to China with some newfound "best friends"—sans parental participation—and my daughter discovers the joys of a good beach read. Even my husband and I are able to unwind with a quiet conversation in complete and uninterrupted sentences.

Before we know it, the air starts to cool as the sun calls it a day. We pack up and head home. This time the backseat is quiet as my sleepy beach bums, with their sun-kissed skin and sandy smiles, drift off dreaming about our next trip to the shore.

At last . . . a picture-perfect day at the beach.

Audrey D. Mark

Five Minutes to Fear

We can only be said to be alive in those moments when our hearts are conscious of our treasures.

Thornton Wilder

Our families camped together once a month, so when the Fourth of July fell on our scheduled weekend, we never gave it a thought not to proceed with our plans. The drive to Rehoboth Beach took six hours, counting four bathroom stops for three children and two women and two men who swore they would lay off the water.

The campsite was five miles from the pristine shoreline and boardwalk. We couldn't wait to dig our toes into the warm sand. Our daughter was seven at the time and our friends' daughters were eight and three. We packed enough toys, beach towels, and tanning lotion to last three weekends.

After pitching our tents and setting up camp, the seven of us piled into our cars and began the hunt for parking spaces closest to the water so that the men would not have to resort to camel-like behavior when hauling our supplies to the beach.

We staked our claim on the remaining ten feet of sand and sent the children to the ocean's edge. Our striped towels and white flesh blended with the thousands of other sun worshipers. Music blared from cranked-up radios while Frisbees whizzed overhead. Fair-haired recruits in muscle shirts hawked their ice cream sandwiches and cold soda while I poured lukewarm Kool-Aid.

From where I reclined, I had a clear view of the three girls splashing near the water. They chased the waves and tunneled into the wet sand, building castle after castle. It took extreme persuasion to convince them to relinquish the sea long enough to split soggy sandwiches with us. Periodically, the men would drop their books and leap into an incoming wave while capturing an unsuspecting child. I could only imagine the giggles above the beach clatter.

After hours of play—and sunburned feet—we motioned for the girls to join us. I packed the towels and lotion while my best friend packed the toys and food. We each had our responsibilities but neglected the most important one. My daughter and her eldest daughter arrived by our side. Their youngest girl didn't.

We locked eyes. Our previously orderly world shrunk to the beach and the thousands of people strewn around us. Instinct jolted us into action. We screamed her name and pushed past bathers and tanners, frantic to find a missing child in a green bathing suit. Each second ticked by as though specifically designed to torment us.

"Angela!" My head snapped as the perfect picture of a mother and daughter reuniting exploded in my vision. I wanted to fall to the ground and weep amid the mass of strangers who had been unsuspecting participants in a drama unfolding before them.

Since that day, I've relived those five minutes of fear at Rehoboth Beach too many times. I relived them each time my daughter hid from me behind a store fixture or ventured out alone in the car after passing her driver's test. I relived them when she was late returning home from dates and when she married and moved to a city far from my reach.

Years later, we relocated to Florida, where once a month we frequent the swarming beaches of Daytona. My husband and I rent beach chairs and an umbrella and stake our claim along with the other beach lovers hoping for a relaxing time in the sun. Invariably, I spy a child dropping his bucket to search for his own cluster of recognizable faces. My heart freezes until I witness the mother wrapping her arms around him again. Only then do I breathe and rejoin the masses.

Terri Tiffany

"I'm keeping an eye on my mom.
I don't want her to lose me."

Reprinted by permission of Stephanie Piro. ©2004 Stephanie Piro.

Cycle of (Beach) Life

Forget not that the earth delights to feel your bare feet and the winds long to play with your hair.

Kahlil Gibran

Every summer it was the same. Sundays, Mom was on the deck early, feeling the air and looking toward the mile-distant Southern California beach. "The fog's burning off!" she'd conclude—if we were lucky. Then she'd say the magic words.

"I think it's turning into a beach day."

My little brother Billy would shout "Yea!" and then he'd dance around in the hall. I'd head to my room, smiling, to put on my bathing suit. We both knew that those magic words meant no chores, no phones ringing, no jobs—in fact, no responsibilities at all. The only certainty behind the words was that we'd have fun. For this afternoon only, we would be the exclusive focus of Mom's and Dad's attention.

During beach days, family ruled.

Mom and Dad were a young couple, dark-haired and

athletic, when they got their priorities in order. Just for the day, they learned to turn their backs on windows that needed cleaning and a lawn that needed mowing. They'd conveniently forget that the car hadn't been washed in a month. If the weather beckoned, it was more important to them to assemble, drive, and trundle everything down to the coast like pack mules, arms overflowing with sun lotion and surf-mats and water bottles. Sometimes they'd have to make two trips. Then they'd set up umbrellas and beach chairs and towels.

As kids, neither Billy nor I lent a serious helping hand. During the packing process, we were too excited. And once we were down there, we'd be too busy gaping at the ocean, and all that sand, piled like the sweetest sugar at our feet.

"Wanna play Frisbee?" I'd ask Dad.

"Dig me a hole, Mommy?" Billy would chirp.

The answers were always yes—yes to these requests and a hundred more, as attested to by my best childhood memories: Dad riding the waves with us on blow-up surf-mats; Mom, taking us on long, leisurely walks in search of beach glass and sand crabs; long games of Frisbee and smash-ball at water's edge; ambitious sand castles, complete with moats and drawbridges, their walls studded with shells; fast-food treats from the snack stand—or just sitting under an umbrella talking. Even into the teen years, our parent/child conversations were always easier at the beach, with the sun smiling down and a million waves keeping a slow, calming drumbeat in the background.

These were the things our parents did with us, every July and August.

The years passed. I got married, and my wife and I moved to Northern California. During summers Mom and Dad would call us on Sunday evenings with enthusiastically told stories: "The water temperature was seventy-four degrees!" or "A big sea turtle washed up on the sand today!" I pictured myself with them again, having shore-side adventures. Gradually I realized I was missing some unnamed but vital part of my life—a lost piece made not only of tumbling surf and the feeling of warm sand under my feet, but family as well.

By the time we had our first child, there was nothing else for it: we moved back to Southern California. A few years later, Billy and his wife and kids returned to the area from out of state. When the weather warmed up, we slipped right into tradition. Our wives learned to forsake summer Sunday projects and just go along with it. Now there was a fresh generation for Mom and Dad to enjoy— new little kids to bury up to the necks in the sand, and teach to throw Frisbees, and tow around on body boards. Our son, daughter, and all three nieces reaped the benefits as well: there's no better way to get to know your grandparents than spending entire days with them, playing in the sun.

Flash ahead a couple of decades.

I'm in my fifties now, and our kids are grown. Dad's in his early eighties, and Mom's not far behind. Both have snow-white hair. Both are a little shaky on their feet; in fact, Mom walks with a cane. But two months a year, we can count on a phone call, early Sunday morning.

"It's a little foggy on the coast," Mom says. "But it's going to burn off. I can tell. It's going to be a great beach day."

They're still magic words. They make my wife and I look at the papers and junk mail that have piled up on the counters. We glance at the shopping list on the fridge and the vacuum, standing neglected in the corner. And then— just for the day—we turn our backs on it all and drive down to meet them.

My wife and I do most of the work now. We play the pack mules, carrying down their chairs, umbrella, and towels, along with our own stuff. Dad's job is to steady Mom as she ambles along (she's doing better now with her walking: two years back, we had to push her to the shore all season in a special, fat-tired beach wheelchair). Sometimes Billy joins us, and sometimes a grandkid or two.

Mom and Dad don't ride the waves or take shell-seeking walks anymore. But there's no complaining. They still eat beach-stand hamburgers, soak in the sights, and talk, their toes shoved into the sand.

The old cues surround us—the coconut smell of sun-block, the hiss and crash of the waves, the cry of gulls. Everything seems timeless, and everyone ageless. The happy sounds of nearby kids skipping and digging and splashing bring back the sounds of our children when they were little—and us, not so long before that.

"Shall we hit the smash-ball?" Dad will suggest.

"Would someone help me up so I can feel the water?" Mom asks.

We wouldn't think of turning them down. After all, it's a beach day—and that means family rules.

Craig A. Strickland

"I need a lot of stuff at the beach."

Family Time

Happiness often sneaks through a door you didn't know you left open.

John Barrymore

"Let's take the kids to Sanibel Island this spring." Just like that, my husband, who needs a much-deserved get-away from the pressures of work (and cold, damp Ohio winters), begins to plan our first family beach vacation.

"That was such a relaxing place. Remember all of the shells that we found?" Smiling at my husband, my heart takes me back over the causeway bridge from Fort Myers, where several years earlier the two of us enjoyed a week at the beach.

The two of us ate late, leisurely breakfasts in our little pink cottage overlooking the Gulf. The two of us lazily read novels in our beach chairs, moving only to reapply our Coppertone or avoid the incoming tide. The two of us, all aglow from the Florida sun, walked hand in hand for miles along the shore.

"Mmm . . . Honey, it would be so great to go back there." But as I look around my kitchen, past the piles of *Clifford the Big Red Dog* books to the crayons, stickers, and coloring books strewn across our island countertop, I realize that life is different now. With two little girls in tow, a beach vacation would be anything but relaxing.

"I'll go online and see if there is someplace for us to stay during the kids' break from school."

"Mmm . . . okay," I murmur, trying to sound noncommittal. "We might need something bigger this time, though. I don't think a little cottage will be roomy enough for the girls and all their gear."

Visions of suitcases bursting at the seams with swim diapers, wipes, and baby sunblock cloud my enthusiasm. *Will our bags even fit all the clothes we will need for seven days? With sand in everything, the girls will need more than one outfit per day. And what about the laundry? Potty accidents and the inevitable spilled milk will create a very real need for a good washer and dryer. So much for my quaint beach cottage.*

Begrudgingly, I agree to a family-size condo, complete with laundry facilities and kitchenette. Our girls, aware of upcoming adventure, are abuzz with excitement. Like little bees, they flutter about the house, donning new sun hats and flip-flops. "We are going to build big sand castles with Daddy!" my youngest beachcomber shouts, nearly hitting me with an exuberant swing of her new blue sand pail. "Can we go swimming in the ocean every day?"

Smiling, I put on a happy face, despite a nagging headache. Board games (in case of rain), stuffed animals, and nighttime storybooks are jammed into already overstuffed bags. Picking up one of my chick-lit novels, I shake my head and return it to my nightstand. This is a family vacation; I guess those lazy days of beachside reading are a thing of the past.

Rays from the southwest Florida sun soon welcome us to our beach home. Sanibel Island is all that I remember— palm fronds waving in the warm breeze along miles and miles of nothing but cool, white sand. Opening the sliding glass doors of our condo, I inhale the salty sea air. Waves roar alongside families playing on the sand. *Maybe I should give beach life a chance.* Shedding our clothes, we change into swim attire before hastily making our way to the sandy shore.

While we walk along the beach, a few sharp surprises underfoot remind me that Sanibel is nicknamed "Shell Island." "Mama, here is a pretty pink one," my three-year-old marvels as she plink, plinks shell after shell into her blue bucket. Bent over in the famous "Sanibel Stoop" position, we scoop nets into the cool blue water, bringing in colorful treasures for our collection.

Just like that, we develop an island rhythm, a routine that involves heading to the beach each morning after breakfast, just in time to discover the treasures of low tide: bountiful shells and egg casings left behind by mollusks. After my husband helps the kids create the world's biggest sandcastle, complete with a water-filled moat, the girls play contentedly for hours, happy to have a playhouse for their "Little People" dolls. With time to myself, I recline in my beach chair and begin a romance novel. (Who knew that our condo would have a bookshelf full of good beach reads?) Time, measured only by the ebb and flow of the tides, seems of little importance. We head inside only for a quick sandwich; often we pack a cooler so we can lunch right on the sand.

Riding boogie boards in the water, my girls squeal in delight as they ride the tides into shore. "Mama! Mama! Guess what?" My six-year-old, all drippy from her swim, comes running toward my beach chair. "We saw a dolphin jump right out of the water! Come quick so you can see it!"

Jumping up, I grab each of my daughters' hands and run toward the water. Sure enough, another dolphin rises above the crashing waves, putting on quite a show just for us. "Cool!" my girls shout, obviously more than a little excited.

Squeezing my daughters' hands, I look up to see my husband, his arm around my shoulder, grinning ear-to-ear. "Let's take a little walk along the beach," he suggests. "Maybe we can see more dolphins. Girls, don't forget your shell nets and pails."

As the four of us walk hand in hand along the shore, sand seeping between our toes, I spot a row of small pink cottages. "Look, there is where it all began," I smile, remembering that romantic beach vacation from years past.

"Yeah, but we have so much more now," my husband muses, his arms heavy laden with shell-filled pails that the girls have tired of carrying.

Laughing, I realize that we indeed do have so much more: more fun, more laughter, and a family with whom to share our love of the beach.

Stefanie Wass

$\overline{2}$

SUNRISE/SUNSET:
CREATING SPECIAL MOMENTS

*Guard well your spare moments. They are
like uncut diamonds.*

Ralph Waldo Emerson

One More Wave

I wasn't thrown out of the house as a kid, but during the lazy days of summer you wouldn't find me at home. I lived on the beach. Nothing could have been better. The beach was everything good: freedom from the chores of daily existence; warm, gentle breezes; waves to ride back to the beach; sand to play games in; and seclusion, in the midst of a crowd, that promoted freedom of the mind, body, and spirit. The beaches were much smaller when I was a kid, so they were more crowded than today. That didn't matter. We still played running bases with a tennis ball and tried to tag the runner out before he reached base. Errant throws usually ended up on a sunbather's blanket, sometimes hitting the person, but that wasn't my problem. I had to retrieve the ball, and in my haste to do so, I would deposit unwanted sand on their blanket and further annoy the sun worshiper. If I got the base runner out, it was worth the verbal abuse. If the sunbather came after us we hightailed it down to the water, jumped in, and had a catch skimming the ball along the surface of the water.

We also built intricate sand castles along the water's edge with protective walls to keep the water away from our castle. As the tide came in, we built bigger protective walls, but we always lost the battle. It didn't matter. We just moved on to another game.

The beach also provided us with a free sauna. It was the sun-warmed sand to flop on and heat up a body made cold by the ocean. In the process it changed those wrinkled fingers back to normal and shed the body of all the goose bumps collected from an hour of energized horseplay in the ocean. It turned blue lips pink again, a signal that it was time to leave the warmth of the sand, run to my ocean, and dive in. Experience guided us so that we reached the right speed, choose our perfect wave, and dove over it with the grace and composure of a carefree dolphin.

Finally, it was a chance for me to attack my buddies in the water, without making it obvious, by going beneath the surface and pulling them under and then swimming away. The best game of all was the piggyback fights in waist-high water with as many kids as were willing to risk it. We would attack the enemy and dethrone the opponent from the shoulders of his carrier. The last team standing was the tired victor.

Fun, but dangerous, was skimming. One would throw a round, thin board along the surface of extremely shallow water as it reached the beach. Jumping on the board we would try to maintain our standing position as we skimmed along the surface of the water. If you lost your balance or if the front edge of the board dug in the sand you would be sent flying totally out of control. It was worth the challenge and the danger.

But riding the waves was my favorite fun thing to do. Today boards are used, but when I was a youngster you used your body as the board. We perfected the art of selecting the "perfect wave" and riding it for several hundred feet, right up onto the dry beach. We mastered the ability to change directions at the last split second. To this day I can still remember the panicked look on the bathers' faces as we just skimmed by them, much to our enjoyment and much to their fright. It was the high of the day to end up on the dry beach. I would lay there savoring my victory for a few moments before getting up and charging into the water again to conquer another wave. It was always just "one more wave" that got me in trouble as I rushed home—wet, barefooted, and full of sand—trying to beat Mom's five o'clock deadline for supper.

As with everything in life, there was a downside to living on the summer beach. Sunburns, blowing sand, other bratty kids kicking sand on you, and the dangers of rip tides carrying you out to sea or waves slamming you into the ocean bottom were a few. But the worst intrusion was people invading the serenity of my existence as I dozed off while lying on the beach with the warm sand contoured around my body and my mind full of the fantasies of my own summer beach.

To me, the beach is everything good, whether you are seventeen or in your seventies, as I am now. In my later years I find that it still draws me into its world of escapism. I no longer spend time on the beach in the summer because of the strong sun and the crowds, but I do visit my old hideaway in the other seasons.

Now it is fall and the transition begins. The summer bennies have returned to their winter homes away from the shore while the parking meters and the lifeguard benches have retreated to their winter storage locations. The boardwalk concessions are still holding their ground, but they are boarded up for the long winter hiatus. Nature is taking control again.

My solitary, quiet, and uneventful walks along the edge of the water, protected with warm clothing to buffer me from the cold winds and the distant sun, still stimulate my body and my mind. They are a respite from the busy world of details and demands. When I walk on my beach now, I am enveloped in an aura of peace and serenity. My spirit, my soul, is strangely warmed in spite of nature's cold temperatures. I know life is still worth living. The simple things of life always bring me back to this realization: Life is good. My beach of decades ago, with all its activities of youth and excitement, beautifully meshes with my beach of today, with my deeper appreciation of its quietness and reassurance. As I walk along examining and picking up the fascinating shells by the water line, I am reminded that now is all I have. Now is all I need.

George H. Moffett

A Wave of Joy

"This is the best day of my life," Joy said as we hauled our surfboards up the beach. I knew exactly what she meant because surfing changed my life, too. It's hard to put into words what the simple act of riding a wave can mean to a person, but I'll try.

Surfing is a metaphor for life. Many people say, "I'll be happy as soon as . . . ," and they finish the sentence with "I get a raise, buy a house, lose some weight" and so on. The truth is, the pursuit of those goals is the reward. Surfers always talk about the perfect wave, but some of the most enjoyable rides come in less-than-perfect conditions. Besides, a good ride lasts less than a minute, but the pursuit of a wave can take all day—and what a great day it is because you are at the beach.

I could tell that Joy "got it" when it came to surfing, even though she was only ten years old. When she first stepped into my surf shop you could see it in her eyes. She was stoked.

Her mom came up to the counter and said rather dejectedly, "My daughter says she wants to learn how to surf. I'm not happy about it, but I'm going along with it because I know it's just a phase."

They say the customer is always right, so I didn't dare correct her and tell her the truth. Surfing is not a phase; it's a lifestyle. I should know; I own a surf shop.

I took the time to show Joy all the surfboards that would be a good fit for her, as well as some of the accessories that went with them. As I did this, something occurred to me. Here I was cooped up in my shop and this girl was going surfing. That's when I blurted out, "How would you like a free surfing lesson?"

"Really!" Joy replied.

"For free?" her mom asked.

"Yes," I said. "With each board you buy you get a free surfing lesson." I was making this up on the fly because I wanted to get out in the water.

"We'll take it," the mom said.

"Can we go now?" Joy asked.

I looked at the mom and said, "Absolutely."

In my mind, there is nothing better than spending the day surfing—except teaching someone else how to surf. I was a little nervous conducting my first impromptu surf lesson, but once I realized I had been surfing since *I* was ten, it seemed like this was meant to happen. The first thing I did when we got to the beach was point out the different colors in the water and what that meant—a sandy bottom creates a lighter coloring while a reef leaves the ocean looking darker and so on. We talked about what makes a wave break and where to be in order to catch it. We spent an hour in the sand (the classroom) before we even got in the water. Joy loved every minute of it.

We waded into the shallow water and spotted a stingray and leopard shark nearby. "Shuffle your feet," I said.

"That was so cool. I saw a shark," Joy gushed.

I wondered how she would react to the dolphins that ride the waves at this particular spot.

It didn't take long. "Did you see that?" she said as two

dolphins darted in and out of a wave not more than a few yards from us.

"Those dolphins have it made. They get to surf all day," I said.

"They are so lucky," Joy replied.

So far my first surf lesson was going great. All the time I took explaining how waves broke and how to paddle over, around, and under them had paid off—Joy had made it out past the surf with ease. Once we were beyond where the waves were breaking we were able to sit on our boards and talk. "Are you ready to ride your first wave?" I asked Joy.

"Oh yeah, but I kinda like just sitting here, too," she said.

"I know. It's peaceful," I pointed out.

Joy then began telling me about everything going on in her life.

As luck would have it, a great wave was approaching us. "Joy, are you ready?" I asked. She nodded. "Okay, start paddling for this wave and stand up once you've got it."

Joy not only caught the wave perfectly, but she rode it all the way to shore. I caught the next one and rode it in. Joy was jumping up and down on the sand, screaming with excitement.

"That was so gnarly!" she said.

"Great wave," I replied. "You can now surf."

We spent the rest of the day surfing together, and when we were done I knew Joy was hooked. I also knew I was hooked on teaching people how to surf.

So when Joy said, "This is the best day of my life," I answered back with, "Me, too."

Lee Silber

The Treasure

Night's darkness is the bag that bursts with the gold of the dawn.

Rabindranath Tagore

"Eric, do you want to go look for shells?"

My youngest popped his head up from under the sheet and rubbed the sleep from his eyes. "What time is it?"

"About 6:30," I whispered.

He sat up and swung his legs over the edge of the bed. "Is anyone else going?"

"No. They're all still asleep."

It was the last day of our annual family beach vacation. My husband and other two children preferred to sleep in after staying up late each night, unlike my fellow morning buddy, Eric.

"Okay. I'll go. Don't leave yet."

"I won't," I assured him. "I'll wait on you."

My eight-year-old threw on shorts and a T-shirt faster than ever. We headed out the beach house door, down the back stairs, past the pool, and onto the beach. I kicked off my flip-flops and waited while he removed his sandals.

Other early-morning risers dotted the shoreline. With shoes in hand, we squished our toes through the soft sand and walked toward the water's edge to begin our hunt.

"Maybe we'll find a sand dollar, Mommy."

"Maybe. I've wanted to find a whole one for a long time. I've looked, but only found lots of pieces."

He looked up at me. "If I find one, I'll give it to you."

I smiled while the hint of tears began to form in my eyes. His tender heart brought him out this early in search of something for me. Now my quest had become his.

While we walked and searched, we talked about his friends, his brother and sister, school, and dreams he'd kept. The conversation stopped whenever he found a piece of a sand dollar.

"Is this one?"

"Yup, sure is." I added it to the growing collection of pieces he already found. With my other hand, I tousled his hair and rubbed his back, trying to avoid getting sand from my flip-flops all over him. "It's amazing that you just learned what a sand dollar looked like a few days ago, and now you can spot pieces of them better and faster than anyone."

He beamed. "Maybe we'll find a whole one since we got up early."

"Maybe, honey." I was hopeful, but the longer we looked, the more I doubted.

An older lady walked up to us. "Here," she said, handing us a beautiful round shell with spirals on it. "I collect these. They're called shark's eyes. I just love them."

Eric and I examined the shell. The spirals spun inward to form an eye in the colorful center.

"That's cool," Eric whispered in my ear.

"Yes, it is cool," I repeated loudly for the lady. "Thank you."

Soon he and I were back on our quest with the new discovery, chatting happily. I picked up a few tiny shells because they were cute, flawless, and easy to carry.

"We should have brought a bucket. Why didn't we think of that?" I asked, while trying to balance all the shells in my left hand.

He giggled after looking at the overflowing pile. "If we find a whole one, we won't need all of those pieces anymore. That'll make it easier to carry."

We continued down the beach toward the end of the island. At a patch of larger rocks, we stopped to scour the area for more treasure. With one foot on a large rock and the other in the shallow water, I searched.

Suddenly, I heard Eric ask again from the flat beach area, "Is this one?"

I turned and looked down at his open hand, expecting to see another piece like the others. My eyes grew big and my mouth might have fallen open. "Oh, my gosh, Eric. You found one. You found a whole sand dollar!"

His blue eyes danced with excitement, and he smiled like it was Christmas. He showed me where he found it, and then we studied it carefully. The grayish-brown wafer fit perfectly on my palm. Packed sand covered most of its star design on the top, leaving only four outside slits and one inner slit visible, but to us it was absolutely perfect.

I handed it back to him. "It's hard to find a whole one because they break so easily. That's why this is such a treasure you've found."

He pushed his hand with the sand dollar toward me. "You can have it."

He did it to me again. Tears welled in my eyes. I swallowed hard. "No, honey, thank you, but you found it. You should keep it."

After a few more rounds of trying, he relented. "Okay, I'll help you find another one."

I smiled, knowing the odds of finding another one were

slimmer than finding the first one. He insisted on carrying the treasure, being careful not to crush it. I made sure to tell every other shell seeker we came across about his discovery. He proudly held out his hand with the sand dollar for everyone to see. My shy little guy even answered the same question again and again for the impressed adults.

"I just found it on top of a pile of shells," he declared.

As we put on our shoes to go back for breakfast, Eric said, "You can leave those other pieces of sand dollars somewhere. Another person might find them and think they found a great treasure like I did."

I left them there, thinking about my son's treasure and the one he was leaving for others to find. Suddenly my shell-seeking desire seemed insignificant. Walking with his sandy hand in mine, I knew that sharing that morning with him was a far greater treasure than any whole sand dollar ever could be.

Paula F. Blevins

Only at the Beach

All that is good in man lies in youthful feeling and mature thought.

Joseph Joubert

It all began with the leopard bathing suit. We lived in an apartment that always seemed too small for the four of us in our family. I was not happy in the high school I attended nor in the neighborhood where I lived. And at that time in my life, I was not happy with myself most of all. I was shy and unsure. I did not like my body or my face.

Until I reached the beach, that is. Every summer, with what little money we had, we would rent a room at the shore. In that room would be my brother and I, Mother, and Father. There was always one of us on a cot somewhere in a corner. But it was worth it all—sharing bathrooms with people we never knew before, listening to intimate conversations through the walls, and trying to get along in a community kitchen.

None of that mattered when I reached the beach. This particular summer, I had bought a one-piece leopard bathing suit. It seemed to feel comfortable on my body the moment I tried it on. It gave me curves I never knew I owned. I had long blonde hair at the time and wore on one arm a gold bracelet that clung not to my wrist, but halfway up my arm. The effect was dramatic.

Nowhere else could I be this daring but on the beach. In my mind, I dropped the personality that proved disappointing in the winter and acquired one that surprised even me. She arrived on the scene each summer as a mystery to everyone around her. *She was brave and daring and coy and seductive. The gold bracelet announced all of this, along with the leopard bathing suit.*

There were many boys who admired what was in the suit. Of course they did not know a shy girl also lived there. Every moment was cherished on the beach. The blankets spread out around us—the radios propped up, the posing and primping and sunbathing with a generous collection of young men arriving and leaving the blankets. We lived our fantasy, at fifteen, sixteen, and seventeen years old, having left our real lives behind. Only on the beach could we become anything we dared. The moment we stepped on the sand, we were transformed for the summer.

There were romantic meetings beneath the boardwalk, promises made and broken, beach parties beneath the stars, with long walks and long talks. We always sat in the same place, as if a spot of beach were reserved for us. And sometimes, even in the rain, we would be there, covered by our blankets. On the last weekend of summer, we would cry as if our hearts were broken. They were. For all of us knew that we would have to return to the realness of our lives and wait patiently until next summer.

Only a few days ago, some fifty-five summers later, a man surprised me with a visit. We had not seen each other for many years. We talked of past summers, of our shared memories of the beach and then he said, "I'll never forget that leopard bathing suit and that gold bracelet on your arm." And then he laughed. "You wouldn't have that bathing suit around, would you?"

I did not tell him, but of course I did. It was invisible to his eyes and others, but I was wearing the leopard bathing suit as always. Every summer.

Harriet May Savitz

"You get to a certain age, and, last year's swimsuit is good enough!"

My Father's Oldsmobile

Those who say you can't take it with you never saw a car packed for a vacation trip.

Unknown

Every hot summer Sunday of my childhood we headed for the beach in Dad's Oldsmobile.

Mom would start cooking the "picnic" at 5 AM. She would make fried chicken, corn beef sliced in thick slabs, several pounds of homemade potato salad, fresh tomatoes sweet and ripe from our neighbor's garden, and peaches and plums lovingly chosen one at a time by Auntie Bella, along with Devil Dogs and Snickers "for extra energy," Mom said. A dozen hard-boiled eggs just in case. Everything got tenderly packed into two round, metal Scotch-plaid coolers, the latest thing.

Dad backed the Olds up to the back porch door, its chrome hood ornament, wide whitewalls, and soft gray curves still sparkling from a new wash. Between mouthfuls of Cheerios, we helped him carry out chairs, blankets, straw bags filled with towels and clothes, and the orange-and-green-striped umbrella with one corner bent up from a previous gust. Everything was methodically loaded into the open trunk and topped off with two huge black inner tubes. Dad said he had a "system." And truth be told, if Mom had asked him to pack the swing set, he could have made it fit.

Finally he loaded us, like a human crossword puzzle—Mom, Dad, and Auntie, single layer up front—my brother, sister, and I, with a friend for each, double layer in the back—and the two coolers tightly impacted under our legs, and we were off!

The Olds rolled down the driveway out of the yard, and soon we were passing through downtown and onto the main highway. Everyone was chatting in a state of high excitement. At the halfway point we stopped for our picnic in a grove of tall pines that smelled wonderful. Mom always said that fresh air made you hungry, as she proudly passed out endless servings of food to her starving baby birds. And then it was off to the beach.

When we arrived, the grown-ups set up the chairs and blankets while the kids raced for the water. Time floated between sand and sea on our salty air playground. Once in a while Mom would insist that my sister was turning blue and called her out of the water. She would sit, teeth chattering, wrapped in several large striped beach towels, just her red curly hair sticking out like a burning bush. Then back in the water she would go, with Mom pleading after her to put on suntan lotion. By late afternoon and many cries of "just one more swim," it was time to head for home.

Traffic was slow as we strained our eyes for the orange roof of the Howard Johnson's take-out stand. Finally we rolled to a stop on the gravel parking lot and raced to save a picnic table. Dad would get in line and return loaded down with bent cardboard holders full of hot dogs, burgers, fries, and drinks. Gone in a blink, he would then get back in line, with six helpers, for ice cream cones. Sometimes he made a third trip when a scoop got accidentally licked onto the ground.

As we sang rounds going home, Dad would sail the Olds into the final rotary. My sister, brother, and I would give each other secret looks as he went once completely around, twice completely around—tipping and squealing, we would yell, "Again, Daddy, again," and with Mom and Auntie Bella begging him to stop, the captain of that happy ship would sail us around one more time.

It was a perfect day!

Avis Drucker

"And here's the towels, and some books and
magazines and food and . . . whoops, the kitchen sink!
Forgot I packed it!"

Day Trippin'

I have no excuse. It was one of those mornings when the sunshine shimmers through the window like a thousand pixie sun dancers and all things seem possible. We were going on a six-hour, round-trip, one-day excursion with the family.

We woke up the teenagers, walked the dog, fed the cats, woke up the teenagers again, piled a few necessities (pillows, blankets, books, games, food, drinks, two changes of clothing and shoes to match, enough electronic equipment to overload the capacitors in Silicon Valley) in the family high-mileage, fuel-efficient Conestoga, woke up the teenagers again, and an hour and a half after our new idea was born, jumped in the car and drove to the corner for breakfast.

"Tell me again why we're doing this?" said Kid Number One, fourteen years old. Nothing makes sense to him except Biggie Fries and Crazy Taxi.

"It's a family thing. We're going to Charleston. We'll have fun."

"I can have fun here." Kid One thinks fun spurts from his PlayStation controller like water from a SuperSoaker.

"We're going to the beach. There are girls."

"Girls are dumb."

"Says the kid who keeps the past ten years' *Sports Illustrated* swimsuit issues in a safety deposit box under his bed?"

Kid One ponders this security breach while he peels open the wrapper on his third biscuit.

Kid Two comes to life at the mention of the beach. "Do I have to wear my swim trunks?" he whines. "They give me a supersized wedgie." Kid Two is twelve, but qualifies as a teenager because he could capture first place in a world-wide pouting contest using just one lip. He is breakfasting on French fries because he doesn't eat anything that has crust.

"Well, you can't wear your shorts because if they get wet they'll drop another six inches below your waist and bind your knees together. You'll cause the beach patrol to issue a warning, and you'll scare the fish. Whales have beached themselves over less stress."

Three hours later, we're in Charleston, as goal-oriented a bunch of travelers as have hit the road since the Swamp Fox turned east on I-26.

"When do we eat?" asks Kid One.

"Does Spanish moss hang on the north side of trees?" inquires Kid Two.

"Do you think there's a gas station with clean restrooms?" queries Helpful Wife.

"Blast!" says a husband who should be concentrating on driving but whips past the beach exit.

All signs pointed to an exciting trip. Especially the one that said if we drove any farther we'd drive off the end of the country. Who says the world isn't flat?

We stopped for lunch at a quaint roadside grill where, with luck and careful selection, you could feed a family of four for the price of a ticket to the International Space Station. "Let's stop here again on the way back home," says Kid Two, enthused, licking sea salt from a twelve-dollar French fry.

Sixteen hours after we left the house, we trundled back in the driveway, weary yet somehow exhausted. We'd feasted, played, shopped, surfed, and threatened, at least once, to clear a wide section of the beach when a particularly cunning wave hit Kid One's shorts at just the right angle. We bore prizes: a fork with an extension handle, a rubber toy on a string that looked like a blowfish in desperate need of a good Roto-Rooter man, bubblegum that turns your tongue blue, a clump of seaweed still bearing copious amounts of sea, and a plastic grocery bag filled with shell bits—altogether a very successful trip.

The toys cost next to nothing, the food was exorbitant, and the look on Pop's face when he realized the next stop was the Atlantic Ocean: Priceless.

Amy Ammons Mullis

The Shiny Half-Dollar

Faith is like radar that sees through the fog.

Corrie ten Boom

My grandmother, aunts, uncles, and cousins crammed into a small bungalow for two weeks, every summer, in West Wildwood, New Jersey. I got an allowance of fifty cents each day. My grandmother gave me an extra, shiny half-dollar. She knew I liked to buy comic books. I put it in my pocket and forgot it was there.

I slept in the kitchen on a cot with coils that made grating music every time I turned. Some mornings, before sunrise, I woke up my grandmother. The bathroom had a spring-loaded toilet seat that would send me airborne, flying out the door. I literally learned how to land on my own two feet.

After about three days of playing jacks on the linoleum, swimming in the bay, swatting green flies, and reading too many comic books, I begged my mother to let me cross the wooden bridge from West Wildwood that led to the main island and the biggest boardwalk and amusement pier I'd ever seen. Everything always looks bigger when you're eight. Amusements were the only things I envisioned. I had my sights set on the roller coaster and the huge Ferris wheel. My mother finally gave in. She let my big ten-year-old brother take me. He had to promise not to run away or leave me at any time. Back in the fifties, most city kids traveled without their mothers.

My brother and I set out in the ninety-degree heat. I felt like a wilted Dorothy in *The Wizard of Oz*; the yellow brick road was the sandy sidewalk and bridge that led to Hunt's Pier, the Oz of my childhood.

"Are we there yet?" I asked Jimmy.

He was the experienced one, trekking to the boardwalk, many times, with our older cousin, Jack.

Once we crossed the bridge, I could see the boardwalk. It was still a long ways off, but the bright lights were coming into focus. We had walked about one and a half miles to Hunt's Pier, the biggest amusement pier in Wildwood. Jimmy and I climbed the ramp that led to my Oz. I was so excited and reached into both pockets to find my allowance. In one of them, I discovered the shiny half-dollar my grandmother had given to me. I now had a whole dollar to buy tickets for the roller coaster and Ferris wheel, and maybe even something to eat. I pulled out the flaps of my pockets and plunk, plunk, onto the boardwalk, both half-dollars fell. I saw them drop between the boards, into the sand below. I started to cry. Then, my brother had an idea. . . .

"I'll bang my feet on the boardwalk, right here, where both half dollars fell," he said. "You go down below and look for them in the sand."

We both realized that he would be breaking his word not to leave me, but this was a real emergency. I went below, under the boardwalk, and began searching. I could hear the stomping above and the clear roar of the ocean. When I looked up, I could see the bottom of my brother's shoes and some other shoes all tramping on the boards. *Boom, boom, boom*; others had joined in my quest for the lost money. I began sweeping the cool, damp sand, determined to find the two half-dollars.

"I found them," I shouted.

Excited, I ran back up to where my brother was standing. There was a crowd cheering and clapping. I was so relieved, so proud, that I found the money. I put my grandmother's shiny half-dollar back into my pocket. I decided to keep it as a found treasure. I gave my brother the other half-dollar to buy tickets for the Flyer, the biggest roller coaster I had ever seen. There was only enough time for that one ride. We had to start our journey back before it turned dark.

Now, fifty years later, when I open my jewelry box and take out the half-dollar that's tarnished with age, the cool, damp sand touches my fingers, the roar of the ocean returns, and the warm memories of my grandmother, like a gentle wave, roll into my mind. And the wind in my hair from the ride that I shared with my brother, on the big roller coaster in the Oz of my childhood dreams, touches my heart.

Dolores Kozielski

Saturdays with Granddaddy

Since I was old enough to walk my granddaddy would take me to the beach every Saturday morning so we could share the sunrise and collect the shells that would wash up along the shore. I felt very special that he chose me to spend this time with him. This became our tradition. As if it were custom, he always wore the same wide-brimmed straw hat, long Bermuda shorts, and a white T-shirt. Two years into our tradition, he bought me a smaller version of the same wide-brimmed straw hat. He said that every seashell collector had to have this hat.

I had the nicest collection of shells. We made all kind of things (lamps, picture frames, mirrors) with the treasures we found at the beach. I'll never forget the way the water would wash over my bare feet, and on its return to sea it seemed to want to take my lightweight body with it. One particular Saturday morning after the sun rose and the sky had turned unyielding blue, we had been combing the beach for about an hour when my granddaddy reached down and said, "Look at this beauty. This is what you call real treasure."

I rushed over to see what he had found. One look and I knew this was quite a find. Granddaddy dipped it into the water and rinsed it off. As he held it up into the sunlight it glistened and gave a kaleidoscope effect of an array of rainbow colors.

"That's a ring," I said.

"Yes, it is, a diamond ring," he said as he put it into his pocket.

We quickly went back to searching for shells, because at age seven seashells seemed to be more important than the discovery of a diamond ring. Granddaddy and I continued our Saturday morning trips to the beach until I was about fourteen. He was getting older and driving was not his specialty anymore, and I decided that as a teenager I needed my beauty rest on Saturday mornings anyway.

The day before my eighteenth birthday, Granddaddy called to ask me if tomorrow I could drive him to the beach so the two of us could share the sunrise and look for shells like we used to do. Just as I was about to protest, I remembered how every Saturday I would wait for him by the front door, and without fail, he was always there. Maybe he had forgotten that it was my birthday and I might have other plans, but I couldn't deny him a trip to the beach. The next morning I arrived at Granddaddy's house, and he gingerly made his way to the car. Dressed in his traditional shell-collector attire, complete with the straw hat, he was carrying a handled shopping bag.

"Whatcha got in the bag?" I inquired.

"Every shell collector has to have a wide-brimmed straw hat," he said as he reached over and replaced my favorite Yankees ball cap with a new straw hat, identical to his.

"Thank you," I said.

On the drive to the beach, we spoke about the weather, his health, and my school, but he never mentioned that it was my birthday, which I thought was peculiar. When we pulled up to the beach I helped him out of the car and we walked down to the shore. The sun was just starting to peek over the horizon, and the darkness was giving way to the start of a new day. Granddaddy started reminiscing about when I was a little girl and how I had to show him every seashell that I picked up, even the broken ones. Giggling a bit, he described how he would answer by saying, "Now that's real treasure," with wide, encouraging eyes. He chuckled harder when he remembered how some mornings I would get so tired of walking, and when my little feet couldn't carry me anymore, he would have to piggyback me all the way to the car. By the time he was finished with all the stories, the sun was soaring into a vast cobalt-blue sky. It was a beautiful morning, and the persuasive breeze made the eighty-five-degree temperature seem comfortable. Far in the distance you could see an outline of cumulus clouds building. Afternoon showers were a possibility. We walked down the beach together picking up shells along the way, just like we used to do.

Granddaddy looked like he was getting tired so I suggested we head back. Agreeable, he turned around and said, "I have something for you." I looked at him awkwardly since he hadn't brought anything with him. He reached deep into his Bermuda shorts pocket and pulled something out. He put his arm around me and continued walking back up the beach. "I've been waiting for twelve years to give this to you," he said.

I was thinking it must be one of those rare shells we used to look for and he wanted me to add to my collection. He paused for a moment, held up his hand, and dangling from his fingers was the most beautiful diamond necklace.

"Remember the ring we found when you were seven?" he asked.

I nodded yes as my eyes welled up with tears.

"I had it made into a necklace for you," he said.

I couldn't believe what I was seeing—the diamond my granddaddy found all those years ago while on our traditional Saturday morning trip to the beach. As he placed the necklace around my neck he said, "Happy birthday, my precious granddaughter."

I never realized until that day that our Saturday trips to the beach were just as important to him as they were to me. As we walked back up the beach I said, "I've missed our trips to the beach. Would you like to come back next Saturday?"

His eyes lit up like . . . well, probably the way mine did, every Saturday, all those years ago.

Stefanie Durham

A Big Fish Story

It was our first trip to Oahu, and by the third day we'd parasailed to unimaginable heights, windsurfed tsunami-type waves, and fought our way through the discount racks at a store with more loud clothing than a Shriner's convention. That's when I spotted the ad for Hanauma Bay, an underwater park where fish will eat right out of your hand.

"Swimming in Hanauma Bay is like swimming in a giant aquarium," the ad stated. Now that sounded more like the relaxing vacation I had envisioned.

Moments later we were on a pristine beach, ready to slip into the warm aqua water, when I noticed the sign offering fish food for sale.

"I'll meet you out there," I told my wife and hurried over to the stand.

"Do fish really like this stuff?" I asked.

"They love it," the saleslady said.

"Hmmm. Maybe then I should buy an extra bag and try my luck at fishing." I laughed. She didn't. So I simply made my purchase and headed out to the coral reefs.

Perhaps it was because the advertisement had simply displayed one-inch photos of beautifully colored creatures called tangs and butterfly fish, but as I approached the reef, suddenly the fish seemed . . . too big. I whipped off my mask, figuring maybe some joker had painted big fish on the lens. Nope. *Had they added some kind of magnification filter?* I put the mask back on and looked at my bicep. Definitely no exaggeration there. I stuck my face back into the water. No doubt about it—these fish were huge! And they were everywhere!

A large group of fish began to gather around me, and I suddenly felt like I was in a Rick Moranis movie called *Honey, I Like Way Overfed the Guppies.* Then one of the obvious leaders of the pack grinned, and I saw teeth. That's when I remembered the food, which I had shoved into my fanny pack. *Could they smell it? Or could they just sense my fear like other wild animals do?*

I began to back up. They followed. I started swimming toward shore. They were right behind me. I swam faster, splashing and thrashing as nostalgic scenes from my pitifully short life played out in my mind.

Finally my chest struck bottom. I tried to stand, but my flippers got caught and I fell. Then two large hands grabbed me, and the next thing I knew I was standing face-to-face with a 220-pound Samoan lifeguard.

"What're you, nuts?" he asked.

"Warn everyone," I shouted. "There's giant man-eating fish out there."

"Oh? You mean like those?" He pointed at two five-year-old girls, petting a school of large striped fish.

"No. These were much bigger and, ahh, ganglike rogues. Yeah, desperado fish. And they were after this." I reached for my fanny pack so that I could warn him about the food. When I opened it, though, a little triggerfish jumped out and swam away.

"That's the guy," I heard a woman's voice say. "He's the one that talked about fishing."

"All right, you're coming with me." The lifeguard grabbed my elbow and I was forced to duck-walk quickly along beside him.

"This is all a mistake," I told him. "My wife will tell you. I'm really a nice guy."

He stopped. "Where's your wife?"

I looked around. Everyone was wearing masks and snorkels and breathing funny. It looked like a *Star Wars* outtake.

"She's here. I swear. We came down on the trolley together. Although now I can't find my return ticket. I think the fish with the teeth ate it."

"You fed the fish cardboard?"

"No. I . . ."

"Okay. Look. I want you to sit right next to the lifeguard stand and don't move until your wife comes to claim you. Understand?"

I sighed. "Yes, sir."

It was about thirty minutes later when my wife showed up and the lifeguard reluctantly let me go.

"Where have you been?" I asked.

"Taking pictures," she said. "Did you know that those fish will come right up to you? And they're so big."

"No kidding . . . So what's next on our to-do list?"

"Tomorrow we're off to the big island to explore a live volcano," she said excitedly.

I shook my head. "Man, this is definitely the last vacation I'm booking from this tour group."

Ernie Witham

"I don't want to go in the water—that man said
the fish were really biting today."

Two Blankets

The years teach much which the days never knew.

Ralph Waldo Emerson

In our family, going to the beach was always a two-blanket event. Aunts, uncles, cousins, and grandparents with two blankets, sometimes more, spread out together "down in front" near the ocean. Mismatched umbrellas dating back ten years, along with mismatched beach chairs with sunken seats, were plopped down here and there, a zigzagged abstract of stripes and aluminum. Piles of towels, clothes, snacks, and brown paper bags filled with pails and shovels loosely anchored all the corners. Finally, coolers in all sizes and shapes were angled tightly under the shade of the umbrellas, and the family compound was ready.

The toes of new babies were gently touched to the cold ocean water, games of Marco Polo rang out from the sea, and older cousins held younger cousins, wrapped together in big, colorful beach towels, to share a snow cone. Uncles built sand villages and nieces stomped them down with joyful delight. And a Cabbage Patch doll slept, hugged in the arms of a toddler under a tilted umbrella.

The shortcuts with wet sandy feet to retrieve a snack or a better shovel or to safely store a one-of-kind seashell would eventually obscure the shape of the blankets. The contents of the coolers would all escape, and a bite of food usually came with a bite of sand. The beach chairs hopped around throughout the day, following the sun's rays, and a trail of pails and shovels would serpentine down to the water's edge.

And after the last swim, our "very large party" would proudly wait in line a little longer for the biggest table at the local seafood restaurant, then dine on chowder and fried clams and hot dogs—our laughter soon spreading to all the tables around us.

As the years passed, the cousins grew up and parents grew old. And soon it was just the two of us. Our umbrella and two chairs were now perfectly matched, and our blanket was always pulled neat and tight, the corners perfectly tucked into the sand. We read quietly in the sunshine, and from time to time glanced longingly at the young families all around us, remembering past beach days.

This summer our family of little ones came to visit at the beach! Joyously, we welcomed the innocent chaos that filled our house. Each day we busily loaded up the Jeep with umbrellas, chairs, pails, shovels, boogie boards, snacks, and children and headed for the ocean. Once again we spread out the two blankets and happily watched sandy little feet take shortcuts.

Avis Drucker

3

LETTING GO

We must be willing to let go of the life we have planned, so as to accept the life that is waiting for us.

Joseph Campbell

A Simple Gesture

I was excited. The day was fine, and the ocean sparkled in the sun as the engines of the old boat began to turn over. It was March 1992, and only the week before I had acted on impulse and booked this last-minute trip to Club Med. Now I found myself on the exotic eastern Caribbean island of St. Lucia. White sand beaches, black sand beaches, volcanoes, rain forests, and deep turquoise water—the stuff that make up dreams. Born a water baby and beach lover, I loved doing anything by, near, in, or on the water.

Only six weeks out of a long-term relationship, I was suffering from a badly broken heart. But I was determined to let the universe know that even though it *felt* like my life was over, I knew it wasn't, and I was prepared to do my part to move on. Now a single woman of forty, the Club Med option to book as a single and share my trip with another made taking a vacation a little more doable. But I'd never taken a vacation alone before, and I was full of trepidations.

I was quickly seduced by the tropical air, the white sand beach, the friendly people, the mixture of French and Latin music, the fabulous food, and the laughter and continuous activities. Although there were only a few other singles there that week, the staff, known as "GOs," were all single. *They're not THAT much younger than me*, I rationalized, *I'll make friends in that quarter.*

And so I did. Although my heart was filled with sadness and loss, the week began to shine with a new kind of magic. I anticipated a lot of different things, and I particularly looked forward to doing some snorkeling.

Twenty years before, I had snorkeled off a gorgeous white sand beach in the Bahamas, and I could hardly wait to do it again. Memories of kicking through warm turquoise water looking for shells filled my mind. I quickly discovered that here, snorkeling right off the beach was not really possible, but every morning at ten, a boat took vacationers out snorkeling. So on the second day, after applying a 40 SPF sunscreen to my winter-white Canadian skin, I arrived at the dock ready to go, along with twelve other eager beavers. My mind danced with visions of lovely, crystal-clear, turquoise water shifting over white sand, where we would explore colorful reefs surrounded by exotic fish.

Our leader was a young man from the island of Eleuthera. A self-starter, Wesley had learned French from the local tourists, and now he shared his engaging smile and fun-loving personality in two languages. Wesley entertained us all.

The old boat motored out on enormous deep-blue swells to the bottom of a great black cliff, where only a few yards away the water crashed into the base. The captain cut the engines and dropped the anchor. We would snorkel here, announced Wesley.

I was aghast! This was not my vision. *Where was the beach? My lovely and quiet turquoise water?* As the boat rose and fell on huge dark-blue swells, I was filled with anxiety. One by one the others donned their gear and with little hesitation jumped in. Now I was not only frightened, I was mortified. The water baby—the beach lover—was scared. And I was suddenly the last one on the boat.

With a gentle kind of patience, Wesley coached me into my gear and waited until I was in the water. The enormous swells surged around me, blocking my view of everything. Although crystal clear, the water was deep, in constant motion and quite cold. I could hear it crashing onto huge, jagged black rocks not far away.

With my heart pounding I let go of the ladder, put my face in the water and kicked along after Wesley, trying to rise above my fears. I longed for my partner of the past four years. I imagined him there at my side, taking my hand while we shared this experience. I really missed him. But he was not there—and never would be again. I was overcome with sadness and loneliness. I began then to talk to God, asking for courage and help with my fear and loneliness.

Suddenly I felt Wesley's hand reach over and gently slip into mine. The gesture was so unexpected, so comforting, that my eyes filled up while a huge lump immediately rose in my throat. Blinking fast, I chided myself, *Don't lose it now, girl! You can't cry into a face mask!*

For the next few minutes he held my hand reassuringly while we kicked along under the surface. Suddenly I did not feel so alone, and I began to calm right down. He pointed at coral here, a fish over there, smiling at me through his facemask. After a few minutes he turned and looked directly at me. He let go of my hand, asking with his eyes if I was okay now. To my amazement, I was, and I gave him a grinning, thumbs-up nod. Twenty minutes later I climbed back up the ladder, ecstatic at my simple accomplishment, with the memory of that kind and gentle gesture imprinted on my heart forever.

During the Friday night sports awards ceremony,

medals were given out with a lot of hoopla and applause
to those who had won events or performed really well.
Imagine my amazement when Wesley called my name
and presented me with a special award for participation,
for simply showing up that week more than anyone else—
to go snorkeling.

Janet Matthews

Mom's Smile

*I cannot forget my mother . . . she is my bridge.
When I needed to get across, she steadied long
enough for me to run across safely.*

Renita Weems

It's an old photograph with bad composition and lousy color. The edges are curled up and brown. But none of that matters. The photo is laced with poignant memories so vivid that when my gaze slides across it, tears prick at the backs of my eyes. I am immediately transported to a place where only good and beautiful images can be found, a place where life revolves around lazy afternoons spent on the beach. In this magical place mothers share secrets with daughters, and grandchildren glean immeasurable bits of wisdom from the cadence of the waves and the soft tones of the women they love.

A mere moment of our lives, tucked neatly into a small rectangle and preserved forever—years before anything bad came calling.

In the photo, the beach spreads out on either side, a fishing dock to the left, one of Calcite's great limestone boats far out on the horizon, and on the right, miles and miles of undisturbed beach. The photo is alive with children and women: mothers, sisters, sons and daughters, nieces and nephews, grandchildren. The lone man in the photo is my father. His shadow stretches long and lean across the restless blue waters of Lake Huron. With immense patience, he casts his line, again and again. My toddler son, his blond curls bleached white, peers across the endless stretch of sand. Mesmerized by his grandfather, he jets down the wet beach as fast as his chubby legs can carry him. His sisters give chase.

A million dancing whitecaps become myriad diamonds, straining to outshine one another. The glimmering trail sparkles on the vast and seemingly endless body of water that starts at my feet and disappears into the sky, where seagulls dip and swirl, calling to one another as an anxious mother calls to a wayward child.

A chaise lounge dominates the photo. In it a woman—my mother—reclines. Mom is spread out in the chair like thick, sweet frosting on a cake. Languid, her arms raised above her head, her legs splayed, pant legs rolled up to expose a goodly length of pale skin. Her arms are bare, the undersides pasty in comparison to the tops. Her smile in repose is tender, sweet, unassuming, and peaceful.

To my knowledge, Mom never owned a bathing suit. I don't recall ever seeing her step into the lake, and never before had she sunbathed. That day, however, was different. It was as if all her cares had floated out to deep waters like the unattended beach ball had done just minutes before.

We are a large family. When my siblings and I were young, Dad was the one who took us to the beach. He sat in the car and watched as we frolicked in the shallows. Mom stayed home to ensure we had a hot meal when we returned. Perhaps Mom was happy for the few moments

of alone time at home in the kitchen, as was Dad, alone in
the car.

On this day, their grown children, with children of our
own, treat them to dinner on the beach. Dad fishes off the
dock, never swaying from his pleasantries. And, for once,
Mom forgets about making dinner.

It is a day of memories, a day never to be forgotten.

My three children are in the photo, and Dad is in the
background, as are two of my sisters and their children,
but everyone who gazes at the poorly developed photo is
drawn inexplicably to Mom's smile. In the photo, her face
is raised up to the sky. To the sun or to our Creator, she
alone knows. Her eyes are closed.

I remember how warm it was that day and how she had
squinted up at me, shielding her eyes with both hands.

"Are my legs getting red?" she'd asked.

My eyes brim with unshed tears as I remember the feel
of her skin on the palm of my hand. Hot. The scalding
tears run down my face. How I wish I could touch her one
more time.

"No, Mom," I replied. "But better put some sunscreen on
before you get a burn." Reluctantly, she'd sat up, the
peaceful smile disappearing, and rolled her pant legs
down, again.

"Save it for the kids," she said, her eyes scanning the
group of children splashing in and out of the water. The
whisper of a smile touched her lips as she watched for a
long, wistful moment. With a sigh, she rose from the chair
and moved toward the car where the coolers awaited.

"Maybe we should get lunch going," she said as she
opened the first cooler.

Now it is my turn to smile. Mom was not ready to relinquish dinner duties, after all. On a whim, I turn my face
heavenward and close my eyes. I draw a deep breath and
search for the special place Mom found that afternoon. It

comes to me easily. Without pomp or ceremony, there she is, smiling again. Tears squeeze from beneath my closed lids, and I fervently pray that anyone who might come upon me at this moment will say my smile reminds them of Mom's smile, that day on the beach so long ago. Tender, sweet, unassuming—and despite our loss it was peaceful.

Helen Kay Polaski

My Shining Star

Barbra Streisand once sang, "Memories, light the corners of my mind." Many of my happiest memories—as a child, a teenager, an adult—revolve around time spent at the beach. I grew up in North Carolina, home to some of the most beautiful beaches on the Atlantic Ocean.

I remember vividly the summer of 1969. My daughter, Tracey, was six weeks old, and we joined my parents and siblings at Moorehead City, NC. My daddy was horrified to see me "strutting" down the beach in a bikini, so soon after giving birth to his first grandchild! I often watch the old movies from that vacation—my favorite scene is the one of Daddy leaning up against the pier smoking his Salem cigarette. When I zoomed in on him, he looked right into the camera and, with a half-smile on his face, gave me that special wink—that only my daddy could give. He died four years later, at the incredibly young age of fifty-four. Years later Tracey put music to that old movie, and when Daddy appears on the screen, "Time in a Bottle" is playing. The tears rolling down my face feel like the tide rolling to the shore.

From then on, my husband and I took Tracey and our son, Stan, to the Outer Banks in North Carolina every summer.

My younger brother, Rick, and his wife, Barbara, would often join us, and he and I would spend countless hours on the beach reliving our happy childhood memories.

I was diagnosed with breast cancer in 1996, and after numerous surgeries, we decided to buy our own home in the Outer Banks.

I work in a high-powered corporate environment and fight daily rush-hour traffic in the Washington, D.C., area, but when I cross the bridge into the Outer Banks, the stress rolling off my shoulders feels like the tide rolling out to sea.

Our beach house quickly became the family gathering spot for special occasions. My mom, who just passed away at age eighty-eight, had many precious times there, surrounded by her five children and their families. If laughter, music, and happiness could bring down a house, our beach house would have become a pile of lumber a long time ago! Daddy may not be there in body—but I know that when I look up in the sky at night, there is one very special star looking down on me, and "he" is giving me that same special wink. I am pretty sure that he has a constant smile on his face, particularly because now that I'm fifty-nine, those bikinis are history!

Susan Allsbrook Darke

AUTHOR'S NOTE: *After nine years of commuting back and forth from work to beach and beach to work, we have put our home in Virginia on the market, and are moving to—guess where?—THE OUTER BANKS, or "OBX" to us locals!*

(Now I will be able to see my own personal "Winking Daddy Star" every night for the rest of my life!)

Harry and George

Animals share with us the privilege of having a soul.

Pythagoras

The day after Christmas, my sister and I started looking forward to the fifteenth of June. That was the day our parents loaded up the cars and we moved to a ramshackle cottage on the bay for the rest of the summer. It was a child's idea of heaven on earth: late nights fishing on the wharf, barefoot days in bathing suits and boats, and meals on a big screened porch under lazy ceiling fans. Every summer seemed better than the last—until the summer we lost George.

George and his brother, Harry, were golden retrievers. You never saw one without the other, whether they were crashing through tall saw grass or chasing bait-stealing herons off neighboring wharves. When they did get separated, Harry would bark until George found him. We all loved those dogs like they were our own, but they really belonged to an old salt known to everyone as the Captain.

One afternoon during this particular summer, Harry

and George laid down for a nap under some hydrangea bushes. After an hour or so, Harry woke up, but George didn't. All of the children, most of the mothers, and even a few of the fathers could be seen sniffling back the tears when they heard Harry barking for his brother. The Captain was almost as pitiful as Harry, who finally gave up barking altogether. But the worst of it was that when he quit barking, he also stopped eating. He wouldn't touch dog food, ignored his favorite doggie treats, even turned his nose up at a cheeseburger.

We were so worried that on the fifth night of Harry's fast, as we ate our supper of fried speckled trout, corn steaming on the cob, and fresh tomatoes, I asked Mama what to do. She said to pray for an angel to help Harry.

That night I lay in bed under the slumber-inducing, back-and-forth breeze of an oscillating fan and pondered Harry's plight. I was pretty sure that angels only dealt with people, and I had certainly never heard of them involving themselves in dogs' problems. But just in case, I prayed myself to sleep.

The next morning after breakfast Mama gave me a sausage with instructions to take it to Harry. I found him and the Captain sitting on the end of their wharf. I waved the sausage under Harry's nose, but he didn't blink. *There's never an angel around when you need one,* I thought. Harry got up and started toward the house. His huge head was so low it almost dragged on the wharf boards, and I could tell he was weak from not eating. The Captain shook his old head and sighed.

A sudden splash made us turn out of habit to see what kind of fish it was. But the smiling face of a dolphin broke the dark water, and even the Captain had to smile back at her. The dolphin made a little dolphin squeak. A deep growl made me look up toward the house. Harry was on the deck, his ears all perked up. The dolphin rolled and splashed like they do, then did something you see trained dolphins do, but rarely get to see done by your average bay dolphin. *Whoosh!* Up she went like a rocket, silver and shining against the blue of summer sky. The Captain and I were clapping and cheering we were so overcome with the sight. The next thing I knew, Harry came flying down the wharf, barking his big golden head off. When he was finally quiet, the dolphin looked the dog straight in the eye, said something in Dolphin, and swam away.

In the excitement, I had dropped Mama's sausage. Harry gobbled it up. The Captain and I took him back to the house and fed him a giant bowl of dog food, then loaded him up with doggie treats.

The next morning Harry was waiting, and sure enough, the dolphin came by. She blew air out of the top of her shining gray head and smiled her dolphin smile. Harry began to bark like he had the day before and got a quick dolphin reply. Then off she went, the smiling silver rocket. From then on, for as long as I can remember, the dolphin stopped by to see Harry every day. My sister decided that this qualified the dolphin as a pet and decided to name her Fishy. But I had a better name. I called her Angel.

Margaret P. Cunningham

Summers at Rockaway Beach

Goodness is uneventful. It does not flash; it glows.

David Grayson

If you spend any length of time at the beach you acquire stories. But the beach is not a story; it's an experience. Time at the beach affects people's lives. My dad affected people's lives at the beach.

In the late sixties and early seventies my dad would take his vacation during the month of August because the waters off of Rockaway Beach, in New York, would finally warm up. We would spend anywhere from three to five days a week on the beach. We would never go on the weekends or on a holiday because of how crowded it was, but we would go most days during the week. My dad would take me, my older brothers (Gene by twelve years and Eddie by six years), and one or two of their friends.

It was funny. Dad told everyone he would take other kids on the block, but they had organized it themselves. They had to make sure everyone had a turn, and the rule was "no fighting" or neither person would go to the beach.

One day the battery on the car was dead.

"Sorry, boys, no beach today. I'll get a battery this afternoon, and we will go to the beach tomorrow," said Dad.

One of the boys sitting on the front steps to the house, with his towel and lunch in tow, said, "Mr. Mac, does that mean we lose our turn, or does everyone get pushed back a day?"

Dad turned around and saw the look on this kid's face and went right away to get a new battery and head to the beach. "Better late to the beach than not going at all," he said.

We got to the beach by ten in the morning. My dad was very fair-skinned and liked to arrive early. We would float, swim, and "ride the waves," our phrase for body surfing. Around twelve or twelve-thirty, Dad called us out of the water. He set us up with sandwiches, chips or cookies, and ice tea. He told us we could play cards or catch with a rubber ball. He then went in the water and swam from 121st Street to 98th Street and walked back. During the walk back he passed many of the kids from the neighborhood. He knew more about who was doing what from those walks on the beach. Many times some of the kids walked and talked with him for a while. It never seemed to fail; he always knew what was happening in the neighborhood.

Now this probably does not seem all that special. But here is how the beach affects lives. We had all grown up, and my mom and dad had retired. One of the boys came back to the block to visit his mother and father, and he had his infant daughter with him. My mom and dad were so happy to see him and his baby girl. As he walked out of the house, the young man said, "This is the man I'll think about when I teach you to swim." His voice cracked with emotion as he quickly walked out of the house. I asked my dad if he heard what he said. He said no, but I think he did.

A few years later my dad passed away. The same man could not bring himself to come to my dad's funeral. But he was waiting. The funeral procession drove by the house once before heading off to the cemetery. There he was, waiting. He ran with the procession, down the block, like a child racing his parent's car. He stopped, and I could see tears on his face.

You never know who or what affects people's lives. But I know the beach had a lasting impact on at least a few lives.

Patrick McDonnell

Oysterfest in Rockport, Texas

The trip to the beach had been a long one—and difficult and hilarious and warm and lonely—and I cried the whole way there. Now it was over. So much was over. A lifetime spent and done, and now the future seemed reflected in the dark sea at our feet.

Standing on the beach, waiting in the night, thankful that we had survived—our marriage, our love—to become something we never imagined; the sound of waves lapping the shore, searching endlessly for wounds new and old, anxious to apply its salty balm in painful but effective healing.

We shivered there on the beach, where we thought no one else would be, but we were not alone. Others had traveled there too, to watch the stars and await the promised celebration, their voices drifting toward us with the wind. Now we watched the boat lights in the bay, wondering if they were part of the show, and how long would we have to wait for the fireworks to begin.

The wind pushed us closer together, gently biting exposed skin, and we huddled side by side. I had forgotten my jacket and he had not, and I wondered vaguely at the dark blue fleece that seemed familiar, but too large, for him—deciding it to be a leftover from the restaurant we had recently sold, a forgotten take-out container, no longer wanted, and did not question its origins as he wrapped his arms around mine, enfolding me in his warmth.

The music from the festival played behind us; the oom-pahs and twangs of tubas and steel guitars mixed with the carnival ride screams and party laughter from the dance floor. We had been a part of that, just moments before, souvenir sacks crumpled into the pockets of the hooded fleece jacket, but now we stood apart and knew that while we could go back, we wouldn't. It was quieter where we were now and the dark hid our faces.

The wind blew colder as we waited for the show to start. Now we turned and faced each other so that he blocked the wind, then pushing me away, he opened the over-sized jacket and pulled me inside, zipping it up around us. We laughed at what a funny sight we must be, in the dark, on the beach, zipped up together in the dark blue fleece jacket, waiting for the fireworks show to begin, trying not to stumble as we sank into the sand. *Wouldn't the children be embarrassed to see us?* Then he said, "I'll tell you something, but it'll make you cry."

"Okay," I said.

"This is your daddy's jacket."

And he was right. It made me cry to remember where I had seen this jacket before, why it was familiar; on Daddy's shoulders in the living room where he always felt cold, then draped over the walker he hated having to use, and finally, laid across the back of the wheelchair that had gone back to the rental store after he died and Mom had no more use for it.

"Daddy loved the beach," I said.

And then I was not the only one crying, as he remem-bered, too, and missed the man who had loved us both so well and for so long. Hugging each other, we knew that we were not alone, standing on that windy beach in the dark. He was with us. And as the salt water sprayed our faces, I licked my lips and wondered whose tears I tasted.

Sally Clark

Searching for Scott

I keep expecting to see Scott's head and shoulders appear over the beach dune, the way they would if he were on his way down to our chairs on the sand. The way they did every summer for two decades, and last summer at this time. The way they never will again.

This beach trip is the first without him, and the first of the annual family gatherings that we are remaking in the wake of his loss. Soon will come Thanksgiving, then Christmas. Then, the year will turn and we'll face next Easter Sunday, the one-year anniversary of his suicide.

I know exactly where we were at the moment Scott put his car in a closed garage and engaged the ignition. We were miles away, saying good-bye after a holiday weekend with family. We didn't know as we drove past the white clapboard country church, where congregants were amassing to celebrate rebirth, that Scott was in his final desperation.

We didn't find out until the next day, after Scott hadn't shown up for work and his boss went to find him. He feared what the rest of us soon came to know; Scott had destroyed himself before the world he perceived as hostile had a chance to.

This man, who was a musician, a father, a husband, a friend, and my husband's only brother, constantly dared life to hurt him. Scott would fling his body into the roughest ocean waves and surf barebellied to shore until he scraped himself on the sand. He took few precautions.

His outward bravado masked his private insecurity. Few guessed how fragile Scott actually was.

And then came the Monday after Easter, and phone calls ricocheted through the family, catapulting a routine weekday into a time out of time. Scott was thirty-seven years old and left two sons under the age of six and a wife whose own mourning was put aside to make sure the boys' world remained intact.

The first blurry hours consisted of unexpected arrangements and hopeful ideas. People arrived in disbelief and gradually became mourners who had to be fed. In the cold light of the supermarket, I allowed Scott's five-year-old to pick whatever cookies he liked best, dumbly believing his favorite treat would make everything all better.

And later, from the quiet isolation that insulates pain, Scott's mother turned to me and offered, "Of course, we'll go to the beach."

No surprise, really. Scott was his best self on the Outer Banks of North Carolina. There he crafted the life that suited him. The rhythm of a town that filled in the summer and emptied in the fall, the inner circle of residents who make the strand their home in every season, a relaxed life based on the vagaries of catching fish in the surf. These were the best of Scott.

He introduced the rest of us to the place, and it became the summer destination we looked forward to all year.

But time moved Scott away from North Carolina. His twenties gave way to his thirties and a mortgage, children, and a career with challenges that intensified as his responsibilities grew. He gave hints that he was in trouble, and told it outright to a few people. But he gave no clue to his brother or his mother; he didn't tell his father. And then, on his very first effort to die, he was gone.

Summer came, and as always, we headed for South Nags Head. I looked for Scott in the blue sky, the ocean, the air. He was already so present in the silences that punctuated conversations, the spaces in a house missing an important resident, the empty chair by the window where he had been photographed the summer before.

Meanwhile for the children, it was summer vacation. They fell on the bed to wrestle with each other, jumped up and down, watched videos, and stayed up late. For them, life was a matter of what was happening today, right now. It was the lesson we adults were struggling to learn.

There were still great meals to be made and shared, days lengthened by a languid arc of the sun, walks along the shoreline that might result in finding an entire unbroken pink whelk.

We were transfigured, scarred, healing into a new unit, minus Scott. This was how it was going to be; he was never coming back. There was no reason to look for him anymore.

Still, we gaped when a cover of splendid, tall white clouds moved in one afternoon at the end of our trip. Minutes earlier, the sky had been an unbroken August blue. Massed around a perfect opening, they permitted an intense ray of yellow sunshine to fall in a solid, focused beam.

We all turned our faces up. I sat down, stunned by the purity of the light. For a moment, heaven opened to us.

Nobody said anything about Scott. And there he was.

Maggie Wolff Peterson

Reflected in a Smile

Hope is the thing with feathers, that perches in the soul, and sings the tune without the words, and never stops at all.

Emily Dickenson

The sun glowed high in the sky as Mom sat on the balcony overlooking the beach with that forlorn expression on her face. My heart ached to see her that way. Tomorrow she would leave.

Earlier that day, all six of us played on the beach. David and I chased the three little ones, while Mom sat in a chair and watched her grandchildren explore the wonders of their first beach experience.

Would she ever be truly happy again? Would we ever see joy reflected in her smile once more?

The baby toddled to the water's edge and plopped into the sand with a splash. He scooped up fistfuls of wet sand and laughed when he threw them back into the water.

Our daughter, the oldest at five, jumped waves with her daddy in water no higher than her belly button. With her small hand in his, she giggled with delight as each wave rolled in and gently crashed along the shoreline.

Mom watched silently with the hint of a forced smile.

Dad wasn't supposed to die. We were all supposed to come to the beach together. After the funeral, Mom took a break from legal matters to vacation with us for a few days. I rode up with her, and David brought the kids down by himself—a twelve-hour drive with children that young.

Josh, the four-year-old, suddenly spied a flock of seagulls. He had never seen these creatures before and was totally fascinated with them. My son, who needed to experience everything for himself, scampered after the birds to get a closer look.

The birds at first scurried away from the oncoming charge. Josh slowed momentarily when he saw they were running from him. He was not dissuaded and decided to try again and darted after those birds like a bullet. The seagulls took to the air, landing several feet away. Josh ran as fast as his little legs could carry him—a new destination, but the same goal. He was determined to get one of those birds.

That's when I heard it. While the game repeated itself, I heard Mom laugh. Although briefly, she did laugh at the funny sight of a boy chasing birds he'd surely never catch.

The sound reminded me of our frequent trips to the beach when I was young. Dad loved it there. Often we'd find him early in the morning or late in the evening sitting on the deck watching and listening. That's where we found Mom most of the time on this trip.

"Picture time!" I called, opening the sliding glass door for the three bundles to rush into Grandma Mongonk's arms.

She gathered the brood into her lap and around the

chair. All three kids and their grandma smiled. Not the forced smile from the past week of pain, but a smile of hope. Better days would come, and they were beginning here at the beach in the reflection of a smile.

Paula F. Blevins

A Toast to a Brighter Life

Once again it is time to pack up the car and travel twelve hours to the beach. We have made this trip many times. This year the ocean serves a different purpose. The night is beautiful, and the sun is just starting to set in the western sky. I gather my family and friends and tell them it is time for us to take our first night beach walk. In my right hand I am carrying a bag. My girlfriend is bringing along a cooler, and my husband has a large rock in his hands. I take the lead—family and friends are walking toward the fishing pier. The sand feels wonderful beneath our feet. The waves are clapping against the shore, and the stars are beginning to shine. Our destination is in sight. We watch the fishermen unloading their gear in hopes of catching the big one. Fishing is not what we intend to do on the pier. We all pay our fifty cents and start the long walk out to the very end of the pier. We feel the wooden planks beneath our sandaled feet. Our gathering awaits my next move. I open the bag that contains items that have consumed me and my family this past year. My husband places the large rock in the bag. With trembling hands and tears in my eyes I drop the bag into the ocean. I hear the splash of the water as the bag starts to drop to the ocean floor. I do not move until I know that the bag rests deep within the ocean to remain there forever. Slowly I turn to my family and friends who have accompanied me on this mission. The words "I hate cancer" come out of my mouth. One year ago the demon of breast cancer invaded my life. Now all of the cancer literature, my wig, and other reminders of cancer lie on the ocean floor. Surgery, chemo, and radiation gone. *Stay on that ocean floor forever, you demon of cancer. I hate you!* The sun sets for the day, the ocean waves clap all around the wooden pier. The night sky fills with beautiful twinkling stars. The stars seem much brighter tonight. The cooler is now open, and someone pours champagne into paper cups. We raise our paper cups and toast to a beautiful night—a night that will always be remembered as the night cancer was laid to rest on the ocean floor. Gone is the day, gone is breast cancer. Let the vacation of fun begin. Our mission—accomplished!

Karen Theis

A Gift from the Sea

The sea does not reward those who are too anxious, too greedy, or too impatient. To dig for treasures shows not only impatience and greed, but lack of faith. Patience, patience, patience, is what the sea teaches. Patience and faith. One should lie empty, open, choiceless as a beach— waiting for a gift from the sea.

Anne Morrow Lindbergh

The weather was freezing outside, but it was warm and toasty by the Douglas fir Christmas tree. Our cats were busy batting the ribbons and wrapping scattered around the room as my older son handed me his Christmas gift for the family. The room got even cozier and noticeably warmer as I read his card.

Whenever I was asked what I wanted for Christmas, I usually responded as many mothers do: "I don't need anything. . . . Save your money. . . . I just want my family to be healthy and happy." My son handed me his present, and all eyes turned to watch me open the handmade gift card. With anticipation, I read his note offering to treat the family to a weekend at the beach at Cape May.

Memories of summers taking the boys to the beach flooded back. Cape May, a beautiful Victorian beach town at the southern tip of New Jersey, was always an ideal spot to get away and spend time together relaxing on the pristine white sand that framed the Atlantic Ocean. With card in hand, I couldn't wait for summer, when we could once again pile in the car and head to the beach.

As the weekend approached, I prepared by digging out an old Fred Penner tape we used to play to make the car ride go more quickly. I packed Frisbees and tennis balls and long-forgotten sand toys. With the car ready to go, my son eased himself into the driver's seat . . . a bonus for my husband, who jumped at the rare opportunity to sit back and play DJ with the radio.

The hours in the car flew by as we caught up on all the happenings in our busy lives. Arriving in the quaint town, we quickly found our favorite hotel, checked in, and hit the beach. After a refreshing dip in the ocean, we basked in the sun and soaked in our surroundings. Sitting on our blankets, my younger son noticed a rare occurrence happening right near the gentle surf where we had just been swimming. A school of dolphins had emerged and were frolicking just beyond the whitecaps. As they gracefully rose from the water and engaged in their beautiful dance before our eyes, I was sure they had come by just to celebrate our visit.

That afternoon, playing games of Trouble and Uno and reading on the beachfront balcony with its peaceful view, the years continued to slip away. As evening approached, we changed out of our swimsuits and made our way to a favorite seafood restaurant. With the sun setting over the water, we placed our orders from the extensive menu of fresh fish offerings and took our time savoring the meal. Afterward we shared ice cream cones that dripped on our clothes as we valiantly tried to keep up with the large melting scoops of cold vanilla ice cream. The evening would not have been complete without an after-dinner trip to the arcade. The whole family played multiple games of Skeeball, carefully stockpiling tickets so we could redeem them for the fabulous prizes such as vampire teeth and snake tattoos.

On Sunday, walking one last time on the boardwalk and dipping our toes in the sand, we took a final look at the calm, clear water. Relaxed and rejuvenated, we packed up our belongings and loaded the car for the trip home. We may have been leaving the beach, but I knew I would keep that special Christmas gift in my heart forever. Time with the family . . . truly the gift that keeps on giving.

Pamela Hackett Hobson

Good-bye to the Ocean

The longer I live, the more beautiful life becomes.

Frank Lloyd Wright

How she loved the ocean!

I can remember my mother striding down the beach with a certain spring in her step, ready to meet the mighty Atlantic head-on.

I can remember how she'd pause briefly at the lifeguard stand to ask the temperature of the water, charming those young men on duty with her wonderful smile.

And no matter what they said—no matter how bone-chilling the pronouncement—my mom would venture forth. It was as if she had an urgent commitment to meet, a manifest destiny with the sea. There was no stopping her. My mother is ninety-six now. "A big number," she says often, with just a hint of awe in her voice.

She no longer frolics in the sea.

Until about two years ago, Mom would somehow manage to have her rendezvous with the Atlantic Ocean. A friend would invite her to the shore, and she'd find a way to get there. Or she'd join up with a bus trip from her apartment building. Or one of her daughters or grand-daughters would help her to the water's edge.

But after a miserable encounter with a broken hip, Mom has sadly said good-bye to her annual reunions with the surf. For the first time in her ninety-six years, she is timid, even fearful. The waves that once delighted her now look intimidating. The ocean is too full of surprises—dips and sudden undertows, crashing breakers that could toss a tiny lady about like so much seaweed.

"No more ocean," Mom said earlier this year. "Not for me."

She said it so resignedly that it made my heart lurch. No drama. No semblance of self-pity.

Old age has made my mother accepting in ways that only the very elderly can understand. She knows that life is tricky. She understands that everything can change in a single moment. And she endures without complaint the indignities of a body that betrays her more often now.

At ninety-six, Mom knows better than most to seize the day, the hour, the moment. She squeezes every bit of juice out of life, clinging more than ever to the precious times.

Nobody—not a single guest—has enjoyed our recent family parties more than Mom. Nobody enjoys her seven great-grandchildren more than this doting, delighted lady who knows each child's exact birth date and disposition.

She had waited, she reminds us, for this fantastic dessert of life. With age comes privilege. But I know that the days are sometimes so long for Mom. I know that the nights are longer.

There are times when her high-rise apartment in Philadelphia must feel like a prison despite its sunny yellow walls lined with family photographs and, lately, the drawings of her great-grandchildren displayed as proudly as Picassos.

On good days, Mom sees friends. On her best days, she visits the fitness center in her apartment building and walks the treadmill. Yes, at ninety-six.

Still, as we greet the golden days of summer, I ache for Mom. I know how much she'd love to be jumping waves in her beloved ocean, bobbing in the surf like a child at play.

But there will be no more "dips" in the Atlantic. No more wave jumping for a lady of ninety-six.

Just lovely memories of the way it once was—down by the sea.

Sally Friedman

September Song

It's an annual pilgrimage, a rite of every fall. And it's one that I approach with mingled joy and dread.

The joy springs from my lifelong love affair with beaches and oceans. The dread comes from the inevitable parting, now that days are shorter and the sweaters have replaced the bathing suits in the bedroom drawer.

I was never good at endings.

So I travel on this pilgrimage to say good-bye to the beach alone. I snatch a few precious hours that seem harder and harder to claim in these days of constant connection with the world; spontaneity is elusive. Beaches and spontaneity should go together.

While I'd like to grab just a towel and dash off, age has brought a certain degree of prudence. These days, my September odyssey means toting along a beach chair, sunscreen, insect repellent, and a sensible lunch. Twenty years ago, I wouldn't have been so prudent.

As I drive along familiar roads with my car windows open and Barry Manilow on the tape player, I think of all the poetry and prose I wish I'd composed about the savage beauty of an ocean and the spell that a beach at sunset can cast on the most impoverished soul.

Out of habit and deep affection, I choose Long Beach
Island, New Jersey, for my annual trek. Proximity counts
too, but somehow, driving for more than sixty or seventy
minutes to reach the ocean takes away some of the
pleasure.

I always end up at the same beach, the one I've come to
know best on this island. I couldn't tell you why I love this
particular stretch of sand and dunes, except that it's familiar and fairly deserted.

The natives on Long Beach Island know this beach, too,
and the few whom I'm apt to encounter on these autum-
nal trips tend to eye me warily. I am the usurper of their
long-awaited peace and quiet after the summer invasion,
the potential "foreigner" who may leave this special place
less wonderful than I found it.

But I brace for the stares each year, and I remind myself
that if I lived here year-round, I, too, would want the place
to myself, come fall.

If history is prophecy, I will spend one hour of my last
day at the beach this year staring at the ocean. I'll spend
another hour reading, one more snoozing, and the last
hour walking.

I will speak to no one.

I will eat ravenously of the lunch I've packed, and wish
I'd packed more.

And I will invariably find some shells to carry back
home with me. They will be carefully chosen, as if my very
destiny hinged on their shape and form. I'll scour the
beach like a pirate searching for booty because these will
be, after all, tangible reminders of a place I love.

One shell from last year's haul sits on my dresser still.
It's pink and fragile, curled around into itself, protected
yet somehow vulnerable. Like the beach itself.

Yes, it's a long, long way from September to May. And
winter looms large.

But for one beach lover, a solitary farewell to the beach will somehow stand as a reminder that it will all be there next year, waiting for me.

And that thought surely makes the waiting more bearable.

Sally Friedman

"I really only get to read at the beach!"

4

TRANQUILITY

The more tranquil a man becomes, the greater is his success, his influence, his power for good. Calmness of mind is one of the beautiful jewels of wisdom.

James Allen

Sunset

The beach still maintains a certain fascination for me, since my days growing up in Washington, D.C. The family would head down to Atlantic City in the days before it became the gambling Mecca it is today. Walking the boardwalk as a child and sharing a common sense of connectedness with other beach lovers set the standard for my love of the sand and ocean.

Early on in my marriage, my husband and I bought a time-share in the preconstruction stage at North Myrtle Beach. This haven quickly became a favorite of ours. My husband and I would enjoy all the amenities of Myrtle Beach and then retreat back to the quiet peacefulness of North Myrtle Beach's surf and sand. My birthday was still several months away when my husband asked, "Have you decided what you want to do for your birthday?" I became quiet as I thought about the impending day. Society has taught women not to celebrate each year of life, but to hide the increasing years behind a bland smile and denial. I was about to turn the big forty. With a measure of resolve I stated, "I haven't really given it any thought."

My husband gave me that all-knowing look of his,

which was actually quite infuriating at times, and said, "How about the beach?"

I shrugged my shoulders thinking, *Why not?* I loved the beach, and so did the boys. I quickly agreed to his suggestion with one stipulation: At midnight the day my fortieth birthday rolled in, I wanted to be on the beach.

As the months turned into weeks, I had some well-meaning friends who could not help indulging in the standard over-the-hill jokes and the "Lordy, Lordy, Bernetta is Forty" signs. So much so that the last thing I wanted to do was to celebrate the day at the beach. I made excuses about why we should not go and assured my husband, Charles, that we would get down to the beach later in the summer. In truth, I enjoyed my beach time too much to start to associate it with a day that I was dreading. Throughout the sixteen years of our marriage, my husband has learned that the best way to handle a situation that I am trying to avoid is to meet it and me head on. Charles decided that if the trip was going to happen, he would have to pack and ignore my protest.

When the Friday before my birthday arrived, he announced confidently, "The boys are out of school, you have the day off, and we are spending the weekend at the beach."

Before I could utter the protest that lodged in my throat, he added, "I invited your mother to come." Not only was the traitor going to force me to walk into my forties hollering and screaming, but he had enlisted the help of my mother to do it. With a reserved shrug I got up and prepared to endure a weekend of false happiness for the sake of those whom I loved.

As we checked into our resort, I wandered over to the window and its view of the beach. As I stood watching the water lap against the sand, a calm that had eluded me over the past few months began to invade my body. I was so absorbed by the calming image that I did not at first hear Charles say, "Coming, hon?" Once inside our two-bedroom, oceanfront accommodations, I walked to the sliding glass door in the master bedroom and opened it so that I could hear the roar of the ocean. I had a spring in my step as I began to unpack. And then there was the singing, which I should never do unless alone in the shower. But my family did not seem to mind as I broke out into a version of Stevie Wonder's "Happy Birthday."

After dinner at a local restaurant we walked down the beach, and for the first time that I can remember since being an adult, my sixty-five-year-old mother took her shoes off and walked down the beach, allowing the ocean water to lap around her feet and ankles. That moment alone was well worth the drive. Not only had relaxing at the beach managed to eliminate a lot of my self-induced stress, but my mother smiled and just enjoyed herself by feeling alive and healthy.

Charles and I walked along the beach holding hands as the boys played and walked ahead of us. As we walked, day began to turn to dusk. We stopped our trek to stand and look at the vastness of the ocean as the sun began to set beyond the horizon. My thoughts drifted to other people around the world, standing, looking out at the same vastness of the Atlantic Ocean. In that moment I felt a connectedness to the universe that can only be described as feeling like God was standing there reaching out to me and showing me the possibilities of grace and mercy born—getting another year older. For no apparent reason I started to cry, not tears of sorrow, but of joy. I had been blessed with forty years of life, and I found myself praying for forty more.

Charles and I walked the boys and Mom back to the resort, and at 11:30 PM we rode the elevator down to the ground floor. We stepped out onto the beach and started to walk in the direction of some lights further down the beach. As the time slowly ticked toward midnight, as if on cue, someone started to shoot off fireworks. Charles and I stood watching as the nighttime sky was infused with shades of blue, pink, red, and yellow. Softly in my ear at the stroke of midnight Charles whispered to me, "Happy birthday." Smiling I said, "Yes, it will be."

We continue to visit the beach several times throughout the year. But there has not been another time when we walked on the beach at midnight to celebrate my birthday. I am saving that for the decade milestones to come.

Bernetta Thorne-Williams

Confessions of a Jersey Girl

Our life is frittered away by detail. Simplify, simplify.

Henry David Thoreau

My love affair with the Jersey Shore has spanned over half a century—ever since my mother brought me here. One look and that is all it took to create a lifetime passion. I have no control over my feelings. It is as if I am possessed by the ocean, the beaches, the boardwalk, the feeling of oneness that comes over me. We are soul mates.

It began when I was a youngster, when we rented a room in a boardinghouse in New Jersey for whatever days or weeks we could afford. We lived in a small apartment in the winter, and there was little money for luxuries. But the shore was another matter. For my mother, it became a necessity. She could endure anything life tossed her way in the winter as long as there was the Jersey Shore to anticipate in the summer. When my father had a problem with his nerves because he lost his job, the doctor told him, "Go to the beach. Swim in the ocean. It will cure you." And it did.

Summertime meant living by the ocean, in whatever way we could, even if it was one room for four people. It did not matter. We slept on beds, cots, and floors—just to hear the sound of the waves or feel the ocean as it swept over us. Nothing could match the magic of a few weeks at the shore.

We would always stay in a boardinghouse. Everyone shared a refrigerator and a cupboard. There was usually an argument going on about a missing can of soup or a grapefruit. Everyone knew what everyone was eating, and when they had a fight with their husband or wife, we could hear their discussions right through the walls. We shared bathrooms and showers, and privacy was left behind in our winter residences.

The owner of the boardinghouse was the boss, and we listened. If she locked the front and back doors after midnight and we arrived late, we had to knock. If any of us missed curfew, we had to stand for a very long time until the door opened, accompanied by a long lecture. But none of us minded the restrictions, for once the day began, we were barefoot and free, running the beaches as far as we dared. It was difficult to explain to anyone who had not experienced shore living: why we had to be there, why we had to abandon shoes and schedules and dive into sandy beds and eat sandwiches that never tasted better, even with sand scattered throughout them.

We would do without much in the winter to be able to afford a few sweet days of ecstasy in the summer as we sat on porches rocking, trading stories, while love was everywhere, just waiting for discovery. As a teenager, I felt it as soon as my feet touched the beach. Romance was in each grain of sand: no matter how young or old; if new or in the memory; holding hands or each other. Love thrived by the sea.

Years later, I, too, would rent a room in a summer boardinghouse as my mother did. I had two young children, a commuting husband, and a big house waiting for me at home. But once summer beckoned, nothing could stop me. I fled to the New Jersey shore. For only there I captured what I had lost during the winter. Only there could my soul burst free.

I now live year-round in a house four blocks from the ocean in New Jersey. I know that every morning if I walk up to the boardwalk, the ocean will not disappoint me and disappear. I can count on its existence, its loyalty, and its commitment. And just as I knew in the boardinghouse years ago, I know the shore will always be an essential part of my life. The love affair continues.

I confess. I shall not love like this again.

Harriet May Savitz

The Sounds of the Sea

Today the ocean roars, bursts upon the old stone jetties uncovered by the relentless waves, and pounds the sand with an exhilarating force. Seagulls swoop down with raucous cries, squabbling over the breakfast delivered up by the tide.

Tomorrow the sea may be calm, splashing softly upon the shoreline and receding with a gentle whisper over the sand and pebbles. The gulls may let out an occasional squawk as they slowly circle, looking like a gray and white mobile in a languorous breeze.

I am blessed to live near the beach and to get my daily exercise. I enjoy walking on the boardwalk. The sounds of the sea are rhythmic and soothing, so I've developed the habit of listening as well as looking while I walk.

I puff along, arms swinging, boards trembling beneath my feet, or occasionally stepping down and strolling close to the water's edge, where lapping waves pack the sand firm enough for a steady pace. Walking alongside the ocean is a delight offering an ever-changing vista and the comforting sounds of the sea.

This has helped me to realize that so often I don't think of listening in the same way as I think of using my other senses, and maybe this is true of most of us. At the beach we see the water, sparkling with sunny sprinkles or glittering with a silvery path of moonlight. We can smell the salt water and fishy scent of the ocean and feel on our skin the breeze ruffling the current washing in toward the shore. And if we can close out the everyday noises so often surrounding us, we can hear in the watery to and fro of the tides the music of the sea.

The sounds are all part of the enjoyment of walking, so there are no earphones for me. I listen to tapes, CDs, and the radio at home and in my car. While strolling I prefer the sounds of nature and the sounds of the world around me.

Today the sea roared; tomorrow it may whisper. I'll be walking, and I'll be listening.

Carolyn Mott Ford

The Penny Jar

May you live all the days of your life.

Irish blessing, also attributed to Jonathan Swift

For us, it was a treasure chest. The large glass jar sat in the corner of our bedroom, waiting for the next time we would scoop out handfuls of pennies to purchase our picnic for the beach.

"I think I have enough," David said as he put the last few coins in the wrapper.

"I'm ready if you are," I called back as I grabbed the beach towels and headed for the car.

A bucket of fried chicken with all the trimmings was our weekly feast at the nearby Siesta Key beach. We looked forward to watching the amazing sunset that filled the sky with vivid splashes of color as if an artist had dipped his brush in his palette and streaked it across the horizon.

This was a place of comfort and encouragement for us, as well as a place of beauty. It had been several months since David had lost his job with no prospects in sight. Life began to seem futile as our finances slowly drained away. Yet our weekly vigil at the beach always seemed to restore a sense of hope as we marveled at God's creation before us. This week was no different than those before— no response to the hundreds of resumes mailed out and the constant rejection of "you're overqualified" from the local newspaper ads. Yet knowing that God controlled the ebb and flow of the tides gave us confidence that everything in our lives was under his control as well.

Throwing the last chicken bone in the air for the swooping seagulls, we strolled toward the ocean's edge. Walking hand in hand, the tranquility of the lapping water swirling around our toes began the process of healing our spirits. A gentle breeze caressed our faces as the sun began its dip into the sea.

"Where else could you possibly want to be?" David whispered, wrapping his arms around me as we stopped to watch the sun's descent. "If we didn't even have a penny to our name, we have all the riches one could hope for right here—you and me, the sunset and the sea."

Karen R. Kilby

It's a Fine Day at the Beach

Living five miles from the Jersey Shore affords us the pleasure of sitting on the boardwalk a few days a week. My husband and I find ourselves a bench with a wonderful view of the clear sky and rolling waves kissing the shore. I am softly humming to one of the 921 songs on my iPod while my husband is staring into oblivion, imagining he hit the Lotto. If he ever won he told me he wouldn't let me know because I would give too much away to family and friends. He would still pretend to go to work so that I wouldn't catch on that we were rich. He forgets that I know the numbers he's been playing for the past thirty-odd years. But this is his time to relax. So I let him have his little fantasy.

Then it begins. Here they come. What are they thinking? They jog. They speed walk. They bike ride. They disrupt our peace. I decide we need to take matters into our own hands. Someone has to do something. I appoint us the JSWWYTP, which stands for Jersey Shore What Were You Thinking Police. We give out imaginary fines to those who haven't a clue as to how ridiculous they look.

We start with the jogger who looks like he will pass away any minute from exhaustion. Not only are his shorts stuck to him with sweat, they have slits up the sides showing more than we need to know. He's guaranteed a fine each day until he just vaporizes into outer space. Not far behind the jogger is the speed walker. She stands so straight, with her shoulders pinned back, that we can't tell if she is coming or going. She gets a double fine because we don't have time to guess her direction. Now we hear the next victim. He's carrying his portable CD player with headphones plugged in, singing at the top of his lungs to some rap song. He—and most eardrums will agree—gets a fine for noise pollution and bad taste in music.

We try to be patient and fair. But some people just don't get it. We watch as the lone couple on the beach is surrounded by all the other beachgoers. These drones search the sand, and the only place they feel comfortable is next to or in front of this couple. No other place on these miles of beach suits them. They all get the "I'm afraid to be alone" fine. Then, parading in front of us is a rather obese middle-aged man wearing a bathing suit, what we can see of it anyway, that didn't fit him back in the 1980s when he bought it. He gets the book thrown at him.

Just when we think we've had enough for the day, we see the little kids carrying their pails or dragging a wagon full of toys onto the beach. Their bodies are so small, you wonder how it all fits in them: heart, bones, muscles, and brains. Their only mission today is to have fun. They don't care who's singing off-key or walking backwards. It's sunny out and it's time to play.

So my husband and I put away our imaginary ticket book and focus on those who have it right, at least for the next twenty years. Then, I'm sorry to say, some of them will pass our way and have to be fined for becoming an adult who, like the others before them, just don't get it.

Maryann Pasqualone

"I took my work to the beach for the day!"

Capturing the Sunlight

Healing does not mean going back to the way things were before, but rather allowing us to move closer to God.

Ram Dass

Sunlight streamed through the sliding glass doors that overlook the ocean in the distance and the swimming pool immediately below. From the small kitchen island, where I mechanically soaped down a pan from breakfast, I looked beyond the living room of the fourth-floor condo we had rented for Labor Day and gazed at the seamless brilliance of blue sky and ocean. Sunlight! That's what I needed to banish the dark clouds clinging to my heart.

Crossing the width of the living area, I slid open the door to the balcony. Laughter from the pool below fanned refreshingly into the tired, aching places of my soul.

I was physically exhausted and emotionally drained. Earlier in the summer, what was to have been a happy family reunion and holiday with our budding teenage girls and my parents in California had turned into a time of unexpected mourning. The glitter of our anticipated

Hollywood vacation had been clouded by the sudden death of my father a week before our planned departure. Instead of celebration, I spent two months with my mother sifting through my father's things and bringing her home to Florida to help her heal and mourn her loss.

Now it was my turn. After pouring myself into my mother's grief and loneliness, I needed my own time to heal. And so we had come to the beach, where I was free to let my mind wander through familiar and forgotten places and reach into the longings of the past to try to draw out nectar for the future.

Suddenly the door burst open, and two wet girls with silver braces shining from their teeth stood before me, their bodies wrapped in beach towels.

"Mommy, can we go down to the beach?"

"We're all going down in a little while," I said, struggling to let go of my melancholy meanderings.

"But we wanna go now!" Julie pleaded.

"Why can't you wait a little? Aren't you enjoying the pool?"

The girls grinned sheepishly at each other.

"We'd really like to go now. Can't we, Mommy?" Laura dutifully echoed her older sister.

My attention snapped to the present. "Why? Are there some cute boys down there or something?"

Their grins broadened.

"Well, let me get my bathing suit on."

They squirmed in agitation, bouncing from their knees up. "That'll take too lo-ong!"

"Okay," I conceded. "You can go down to the beach, but don't go past the condo and don't go in the water till Daddy and I get there."

In a flash, the wet drips on the carpet were abandoned. The door slammed, and I heard wet, pattering feet running down the hall.

That afternoon as my husband and I sat under our umbrella on the beach, we watched two girls tiptoeing into their early teens as they strutted through white sand in new bathing suits. Giggling and posing in self-conscious innocence, they periodically dropped down on the blanket beneath our umbrella to report on the triumphs of the day.

"What a pair," Marv said as we watched them saunter down toward the ocean once again.

The tape in my mind did a quick rewind, and I saw myself at thirteen strolling along a Southern California beach in a yellow two-piece. At a distance my father raised his camera, eyes twinkling and face beaming. The camera clicked.

"Those are two beautiful girls," my husband observed, laying his camera on the beach towel.

Two boys approached our daughters in the water. Demure smiles brightened. The blond boy took the lead, talking, gesturing. They were laughing. Proudly, Laura glanced our way and smiled. I smiled back and waved, but she pretended not to see.

I chuckled. Heavy layers of fatigue and sorrow began to peel away under the warmth of a bright summer sun and sweet sense of today. "Our little girls are growing up," I said.

Marv nodded and pulled me close as the tableau unfolded at the water's edge.

Together we watched yesterday evaporate into today while today danced in the sunlight and flowering of a new generation. Our daughters' dreams were for tomorrow. Ours curled around us in the present and unfolded one by one, waiting to be captured and held close in this singular moment of time.

"This has been a great day," Marv said. "Let's come back here again sometime."

But I wasn't sure we ever could.

Linda W. Rooks

Ebb and Flow

"Why is this happening to me?" I shouted to the wind. Standing ankle-deep at the Pacific Ocean's edge, I wanted to scream—but no one would hear me. I was alone.

I'd just divorced after a seventeen-year marriage. On top of that, I moved from a midwestern state all the way to Southern California. Back there, I lived on the shores of Lake Michigan. The water was always on my right. Here, the water was on my left. Everything seemed backward, including my life.

I thought I'd still be married. Happily ever after, right? Instead, I was building a brand-new life in a brand-new state. It felt wrong, and yet so right.

I looked up at the clouds overhead. They were white, filled with promise.

I heard the seagulls squawking as they swooped around the cliffs behind me.

I gazed out to sea. It stretched out endlessly, seemingly beyond eternity. The water shimmered when the sun peeked out from behind the clouds.

But it was the waves, the constant and ever-flowing waves that calmed me, soothed me, and sent a message deep into my soul.

Life was all about ebb and flow. Some things come to you; some things are taken away. But then more things come to you ... and more and more and more. It never stops. Life goes on.

A couple of years later I found myself sitting astride a low cement wall gazing out at that same Pacific Ocean. Only this time I wasn't alone.

"Here you go," a handsome man said. "One order of fish and chips with an ocean view."

"Thanks," I replied and placed the warm paper basket on my lap. The fish was delicious, but it was whom I was with that was even more thrilling.

"I have something to ask you," he said. Then he put the remainder of our lunches aside. Kneeling in the sand, he took my hands. "Would you marry me? I know I have a lot of baggage, and I know ..."

"Shhhh," I whispered. "Yes, I'll marry you."

As we rose to our feet to embrace, I was facing the ocean. The waves were cresting and reaching for shore. The sun was bright and high in the sky. The air was warm as a gentle breeze caressed my bare shoulders.

Ebb and flow, life goes on, sometimes even sweeter than before.

B. J. Taylor

5

SPECIAL
MEMORIES

*Memory is a child walking along the
seashore. You can never tell what small
pebble it will pick up and store away
among its treasured things.*

Pierce Harris

Yesterday's Future

Fun in the sun in Ortley Beach, New Jersey, had been a summer tradition for my family and many of my friends' families for years. Everyone would rent a bungalow within walking distance of the beach for two weeks or so. Sometimes the vacations would overlap and we kids lucked out. I remember stretching one vacation for almost the whole summer by staying at someone else's house. Oh, not just me, but the whole group of us.

The group would meander to the beach around 10:30 AM and stay until 4:00 PM—eventually everyone would make an appearance. Every day our group gathered to enjoy one another's company like long-lost friends who had not seen each other in years.

In those days no one questioned kids around the age of twelve going to the beach by themselves, for as I recall, we knew our limitations and never thought of challenging them. We were more interested in just getting together, sporting a suntan, meeting boys, and dreaming about dating the lifeguards.

We would bring sandwiches, snacks, and Thermoses filled with iced drinks—literally ready to camp out for the day. Some days we would splurge and buy a hot dog, cold soda, and the best lemon-ice cup at the refreshment stand.

Our days were routine: sunbathing on colorful beach towels and blankets while listening to and singing along with songs from the Hit Parade on the portable radio, playing volleyball, building sand castles, and collecting seashells for craft projects.

On those occasional sweltering days, we would speed across the hot sand down to the water's edge and splish and splash in the cool ocean waves. This, however, was a secret ploy to get a closer look at the "men" on duty, bound to protect us poor "helpless" women, ages twelve and thirteen. Besides, it was refreshing and we were at the beach!

Come four o'clock we would pack up, rush home to shower, fix our hair, eat supper, put on a snazzy new outfit, and head out for boardwalk adventures in the next town, Seaside Heights. Anticipated fun and excitement welcomed us every night. We never got bored because there was sooo much to do.

Amusement rides: the merry-go-round, the whip, the roller coaster, the haunted house . . . and more.

Games of chance: ring toss, dart the balloons, wheels of fortune to win humongous stuffed animals and tiny plastic trinkets, watergun horse races . . . and more.

There were arcades, food stands, salt water taffy, cotton candy, and pizza by the slice.

Not to mention the clams on the half-shell, fortune tellers, and the movie theatre (only one) packed on rainy days.

Oh, to return to the days when life was simpler and safer, and when spirits soared. A time when the future meant tomorrow and the next day's activities were the only major concern—even though we knew what they would be. What a gift it would be to take a trip back in time and revisit those lazy, hazy days of fun in the summer sun at the beach. To rendezvous with those who played such an important part of your life. Review the experiences that made you who you are today. A trip, if you will, that would take you back to yesterday's future. A trip you would not change.

Helen Colella

Eternal Love Affair

We do not remember days; we remember moments.

Cesare Pavese

Sand and the Albemarle Sound were the highlights of my summers. The topaz waters that seem to beckon one to swim and always capture your heart exist along the shore of the inner banks of the North Carolina coast. The Native Americans who lived near the waters and ate the grapes along the woodlands knew this land was special. And now I know it as well.

The Legion Beach of the Albemarle Sound knows me better than I know myself. For at the end of a tiring day, when I walk along her shores, she caresses my feet—but even more, she caresses my tired soul. The gentle wind seems to push me along as I walk out on the old wooden pier that extends a good distance into the water. I dangle my feet into the cool waters and listen as the seagull calls out to the wind.

And I am changed in this place—along the beach where I walked as a young girl. I gaze out at the waters where I water-skied at sixteen and smile as I remember the day I finally learned to let go of the rope when I fell. I smile as I remember all the times like Saturday night dances with sixties beach music. I laugh as I recall dancing the twist as the sounds of the music floated through the air.

I remember the young men who walked this shore who went on to Vietnam. They were so young—so full of life—how they loved this beach! One Saturday they were jumping off the pier swimming far out, and the next week they were sent to war. Three of them never returned home—but this beach owned by the Veterans of Foreign Wars remembers them.

The beach and I go way back; we have a friendship that I realize will always exist. I have changed ever so much, but our friendship has remained basically the same. Yes, the shoreline has eroded somewhat—and the pier has been rebuilt due to hurricanes a couple of times—but ah, my friend has managed to capture so many hearts and hold them forever. It always has been that way here at the Legion Beach.

Yesterday, I took my daughter, my granddaughter, grandson, and great-granddaughter down here. We stood on the pier and listened to the symphony of seagulls calling out to the wind the way they always do, and we watched as the topaz waters lapped against the wooden pier. I looked at them—caught up in the splendor—and I smiled once again. It was happening to them, too. They were falling in love with this place just as I knew they would.

My grandson splashed in the water as he and his sister enjoyed the day. Later, as we prepared to leave, I looked into the eyes of Kaylee, my great-granddaughter, and I whispered in her ear: "Darling Kaylee, someday you will come back here, and you will feel the love of all the generations before you—and you will feel the magic of this place as well. It is one of the greatest legacies I can leave you. It was left to me—and to all the kids who grew up in those special times."

My three-year-old grandson grabbed my hand as I slowly stood up. "Gramma, can we come back tomorrow?"

I laughed as I said, "Why, yes, and for a lot of tomorrows I pray."

God had painted a majestic sunset in hues of violet, orange, and pink. I watched as it reflected off my children's face. I stood there, and I knew that in this life of mine—and on this beach—I had touched the edge of splendor. I could not ask for more.

Marsha Brickhouse Smith

Honeymoon on the Beach

The wedding was beautiful,
the reception first rate,
we left our family and friends,
believing married life was great.

Our honeymoon started,
we arrived at the beach,
our very first winter tan
was now within our reach.

We were given a nice room
on the fifth floor,
a beachside with terrace,
who could want more?

The sky was sunny,
the temperature eighty-two,
the breezes balmy,
their pool was open too.

To test the mattress,
we laid on the bed,
the headboard fell,
putting a knot on my head.

When the headache quit,
I went for some air,
out on our terrace
and into a chair.

As we sat quietly,
watching the sea,
the cheap chair collapsed
out from under me.

There I sat in horror
on the narrow terrace floor.
As my new husband stared,
I scooted back through the door.

My face was red,
my legs were bruised,
my poor rear end
was really abused.

With a straight face,
my husband said,
"Honey you look beat,
want to lie on the bed?"

I did as he suggested.
He went for some ice.
As he closed the door,
I swear he laughed twice.

We stayed inside
the rest of the day,
wondering what else
would come our way.

They always say
things happen in threes,
but I prayed to God,
"No more, please."

We went to bed early,
then in the middle of night,
I went to the bathroom,
oh Lord, what a sight.

Ants were everywhere,
on the floor and the walls,
our toothbrushes covered,
I ran crying to the hall.

A frantic phone call
to the front desk below.
Hubby explained our problem,
the girl said, "Ooh, no!"

She sent an employee
to inspect our room.
While he was with us,
he noticed my gloom.

He asked "What is wrong,
is it more than the ants?
Isn't your honeymoon,
being filled with romance?"

I showed him the knot
in the middle of my forehead.
He asked what caused such a thing.
I said the headboard fell off the bed.

I showed him the terrace,
with the broken-down chair,
which caused the bruises on my body,
both here and there.

A discreet phone call later,
we were moved to the honeymoon suite.
There was no added charge,
now wasn't that extra sweet?

What started to be
our honeymoon from hell
turned out to be fantastic,
the rest went quite well.

If you get a bruise on your bottom,
and a large knot on your head,
you can be moved from a nice double,
to a suite with a king-size bed.

This marriage has lasted,
it's our thirty-third year.
After surviving our honeymoon,
there was nothing left to fear.

Pamela Gayle Smith

"One of the top perks of marriage . . . there's always someone to rub sunscreen on your back!"

Seal Island

Courage is being afraid but going on anyhow.

Dan Rather

Born and raised in Winston-Salem, North Carolina, my husband had never so much as dipped a toe in the ocean. And he had no interest in doing so. I was shocked when I learned that my twenty-eight-year-old future husband had no clue how to swim. Andrew had no interest in ever seeing the ocean, much less swimming in it. He was convinced that he'd either sink like a rock to the bottom, or he'd be attacked by a shark.

"Honey, it's virtually impossible for you to sink to the bottom of the ocean. You do have legs and arms you know. All you have to do is move them."

"I'm telling you I sink like a stone," he continued. "My father tried to teach me how to swim in a pool when I was a kid."

"What happened?" I asked.

"I ended up on my back at the bottom of the pool. Just lying there and staring up at the surface. I couldn't move."

I started to laugh, but he looked serious. My soon-to-be

husband wanted nothing to do with the ocean and the magic it has to offer.

I had to admit my heart was a little broken. I grew up in the Northeast, and my family spent each summer in a Maine beach cottage. Summer vacation was a reprieve from "real life" that I looked forward to each and every year of my childhood. My parents always fought a great deal and never seemed very happy together. However, our time at the beach seemed to make our family a little more cheerful. My parents fought less, and my older sister and I spent time together. At the beach, my family seemed closer; hence, Maine had always been special to me.

Due to some difficult family circumstances, Andrew and I had planned to elope. Sitting together in front of the computer, we searched on the Internet for a special place to get married. We looked at the mountains in Gatlinburg, Tennessee, with its beautiful chalets and open-air hot tubs. We then considered Florida.

"How about Dollywood, Tennessee?" I said, laughing. It was as good a place as any at that point. Nothing seemed to click. I had a good idea where I'd like to get married, but didn't think Andrew would go for it.

The next morning the winter sun was strong and woke me far earlier than I had intended on a Sunday. From the den, I heard the almost silent sound of keys tapping.

"Have you ever heard of Seal Island?" he asked as I entered the den.

"Nope," I said, sliding into the computer chair.

"Well, you'll be there by December eighteenth."

That was in three days. What was he talking about?

Seal Island, I learned, was a little wisp of an island off the coast of Wells, Maine. Somehow he stumbled across it on the Internet, and he had already rented a cottage for us directly on the beach.

"Honey, you have never wanted to go near the ocean," I said. "What are you thinking?"

"That I love you," he said, kissing my nose. "Go get packed."

Two days later, I bought a dress off the rack, picked up two wedding rings, and let my parents know we'd be arriving. Long since divorced, both lived close to where we vacationed as a family. I suppose that it held good memories for all of us. Andrew and I boarded the flight from North Carolina to cold, snowy Maine just in time for our December twentieth wedding. My mother picked us up at the airport, and I noticed Andrew sniffing the air with some interest, like a dog catching a whiff of steak on the grill.

"What's that smell?" he asked.

"Salt air! Isn't it great?" I said, excited to be back in Maine.

He shrugged his shoulders unconvinced, but kissed my mother and off we went to find the cottage. I admit I was nervous. In our relationship I did all of the planning, and for good reason. My husband's idea of a romantic date was combing through the DVD section of a discount store and grabbing a sandwich at a fast-food place.

We pulled into the driveway of a small house in Wells. The cottage was white, and though not directly on the sand, was seated on a low cliff. Salty, misty air enveloped the house. Inside, the owners had decorated a Christmas tree, and it stood majestically in the center of a picture window that looked out onto the winter sea. Standing by the window, I squinted through my bad eyes and asked what was moving out on the water.

"Seals," Andrew said excitedly, wrapping his arms around my waist. "That must be Seal Island!"

We stood together and watched seals dive and swim, then climb back onto the small island to huddle together.

But we had to move along—we had a wedding to prepare for the following afternoon.

We awoke the next morning to a sight to behold. The sea was stormy, with waves crashing against the rocks. Seagulls swooped overhead, their cries reminding me of those special summers as a child. A few hours later, we took our vows standing by the picture window. I wore a simple cream-colored dress, and my husband wore informal trousers and a shirt, set off by a royal blue tie with tiny snowflakes. The white cake was covered with red frosted roses, and sugar-encrusted snowflakes surrounded the base. A few family members took us to a quaint restaurant down the road, where we had our first meal as husband and wife. At the end of dinner, everyone left, leaving my new husband and me in our cottage by the sea. It was late afternoon, and snow started sifting from the sky. Thinking Andrew would be ready for a nap, I went to change into comfortable clothes. He followed me into the bedroom and took me by the hand, leading me to the front door of the cottage. "Wait here," he said, returning a moment later to hand me my small bridal bouquet of red roses. My husband led me outdoors down a winding rustic path to the ocean. I was in my wedding dress and heels still. *Was he crazy?*

Reading my thoughts, he picked me up and carried me over the rocks to where a small patch of sand waited, not yet filled with snow. I watched him as he took off his nice shoes, and then his socks. "Andrew, it's snowing. . . . It's freezing," I said. "What are you doing?"

"I never thought I would want to put my feet in the ocean," he said, "much less in twenty-degree weather, but this is no ordinary day."

And there in front of me was my new husband. Six-feet-four inches, his pants rolled up to his calves, laughing like a child and splashing in the sea. The seals were still cavorting on their island, and it felt like the world was celebrating with us. I tossed my bouquet into the water, imagining all of the memories to come.

Heather Cook Lindsay

"It's the ocean—for you."

Time and Tides

Memory is a way of holding onto the things you love, the things you are, the things you never want to lose.

From the television show *The Wonder Years*

Today my eyes blur with tears as I look at the photographs of my toddler grandchildren on a special Cape Cod beach last summer. Kira, wearing a large green sunbonnet pushed back by the breeze, waves a shovel in one hand and carries her pail in the other, while Luke, water lapping over his toes, studiously sorts shells and stones. Michele, the proud mom, soaks in the sun and the moment from a blanket nearby, while out in the bay, Dana, my younger daughter, sails her beloved Bonito racing skiff, red and white sail tilted, heeling against the wind.

I know I am not seeing clearly. *Isn't this really a picture of Michele and Dana at the ages of Luke and Kira, shoveling and splashing on this same beach? Am I not the woman sitting on that same blanket with my husband, savoring that special sense of coming home that children have with the beach?*

Back in the sixties, when we first went to Eastham, our old black and white Plymouth was just big enough to hold the requisite suitcases, books, pails, shovels, inflatable tubes, teddy bears, groceries, sheets, and towels that we would need for a week in a small rental cottage at the cape. Minutes after we arrived that first summer, we lost sight of Dana while we were unloading the car after our long six-hour trip from New York. Like a homing pigeon, she instinctively headed toward that beach on the bay, and she has returned each summer since. Now I'm the only one in the family who has never gone back.

There was no television in that small rental cottage. Instead, each morning the beach helped us create a new story for that day. Is the tide in or out? What time can we swim? Are the clouds and the wind saying we can sail this afternoon? When it's low tide, can we walk out to the old target ship far out on the bay? If it's raining, can we go to the Visitor Center at the National Seashore? Or can we just read and play Monopoly in our small cottage? Time at the beach took on a new dimension. Clocks were irrelevant. Instead, the tides, the sunsets, and the sunrises guided the rhythm of our days.

As we returned each year to that same cottage, the beach brought returning friends for the children as well. Encyclopedia Brown, as they named him, was a thin, wiry, bespectacled little boy, who each morning excitedly told us about his daily discovery of a sand shark or a horseshoe crab, or sadly, one day, some pilot whales that stranded themselves on our beach. Tall and quiet Walter from Massachusetts came regularly to our blanket with a deck of cards in hand and waited for Michele to come in from her swim so they could play several rounds of Michigan Rummy. Susan from Connecticut was a lively companion for Dana as they swam off the dock or raced their sailboats toward the horizon.

Some evenings meant a bonfire on the beach; other evenings meant early bedtime after a full day of sun and sand and a wonderful, fresh clam chowder dinner. At least one night during our vacation we had an inhibition-shattering, succulent lobster dinner, served on oil cloth-covered tables at the Lobster Hutt in Wellfleet. Afterward we washed butter-soaked hands in conveniently placed sinks in each corner of the room and headed to Orleans for enormous hot fudge sundaes at Dairy Queen.

But by far the best dessert was the rich bay sunset that the beach offered us at night. At dusk the blanket became our vantage point for the dazzling gold, orange, and purple light show that illuminated the entire sky and subtly changed hues each second of the sun's deliberate descent. It was as if the sky dressed itself in royal robes to bear witness to the ritual leave-taking of its majestic ruler, and those of us who were privileged to watch became silent in awe and wonder.

Somewhere during the seventies, we needed my Volkswagen Bug and the big old Oldsmobile known as the Queen Elizabeth to get bikes, the Bonito, guitars, and two teenage girls from New York to Cape Cod. But we didn't miss a summer. Encyclopedia Brown and Walter were still there, only now they talked of college plans, Genesis, and Led Zeppelin. One year Walter invited Michele to his senior prom, and she accepted. The Vietnam War came and went, Elvis died, and Nixon resigned. But we still searched for the perfect shell, walked the mud flats to infinity, and savored the delightfully messy lobster dinner in Wellfleet. And we still raced to get to our blanket in time for the sunsets. The beach was our anchor.

By 1980 we built our own house in Eastham, within walking distance of the same beach. My husband and I dreamed of our children and grandchildren visiting us

there in our retirement. Who wouldn't want to come to
Cape Cod in the summer, no matter where they lived the
rest of the year?

The year 1984 was the last summer I spent on the cape.
I loved the house I had helped design, and I loved the web
of memories of my children that we wove for all those
years at that special beach. But my marriage was over, and
in the division of spoils known as divorce, my husband
got the cape house while I stayed in New York.

Today, I live in Colorado. My daughters live in the West
and Northwest, but they still return to Eastham each summer. Now, as I look at these pictures, I see clearly that it is
my grandchildren frolicking on the beach I knew so well.
My heart aches, but I know that even though the tides of
our lives go in and out, the beach and our family will
remain.

Dee Montalbano

Timeless Sea

I plop right down in the ocean-soaked sand, just far enough from the incoming tide, and begin digging. I use my hands, never a shovel, letting the fine wet grains stuff themselves behind my fingernails. I won't go as far as China today. I'll scoop just enough to make a castle. It all depends on how close I am to the surf. I dig and dig and dig until the underground flow suddenly appears and fills up the hole I created. Magic!

At forty-two, this is all a mystery to me. How does the water come to fill the hole from below? If it's always there, why don't I see it until I dig? How does liquid hold its form beneath solid ground?

I'm sure there are simple, widely known answers to these questions, but I don't want to know; I've enjoyed a lifetime of wonder. Once my pool fills, I set to work, letting the soupy sand trickle from my hand onto the pile of hard earth. Trickle, trickle, trickle . . . my castle grows, taller and taller, until it is time to fashion a tower—a careful drip, drip, drip as the tiny drops of soup harden into chips, creating a delicate spire.

I am reminded of a castle in France built ages ago upon craggy rock, the sea rushing to surround it with the tide. I, too, am a creator, artist, architect, building a cathedral. I, too, have spent a lifetime at this holy task, like the children before me, and so too the ones after me—after I myself am washed away from the shore of this world. Bridges, moats, and castle walls, all crafted by loving hands, until the tide retrieves them, and we begin again.

It is the summer of 1963, of 1981, of 2006. Time is no matter. The salt still sprays in the air, coating the downy hairs of my face. The gulls still swoop overhead; the pipers run to and fro in the surf. The sky is blue or gray or white; the water is warm, seaweed filled; or cold, bringing clamshells to the shore.

My feet are sprinkled with sand—the tiniest specks of gray, black, and white. In the heat of noontime sun, my step quickens, becoming staccato as I dash through the soft, dry mounds of the dunes before they scorch my soles. I am heading toward my car, or toward the music of the ice cream truck, or toward cousins arriving to join us for the afternoon. . . .

My grandmother has packed us peanut butter crackers and lemonade; later, she'll surprise us with root beer barrels and sour balls. I'll watch her mouth pucker, creating hollows beneath her cheekbones as she studies the crossword puzzle with a sharpened pencil behind her ear.

When we return home, we will shower outside, and she will powder our bodies before feeding us a dinner of fried tomatoes and corn (that we shucked ourselves in the backyard). Our hair, freshly combed, will be damp as we crawl into bed, and someone will protest that the sun is still shining. "It's after eight," she'll answer, firmly tucking the covers around us. The hum of the air conditioner and the faint call of gulls will be our lullaby as we sink into sleep, burrowing our way back into the timeless sea—like the tiny purple clams uncovered in our digging.

Kelly Salasin

The Treasure Buried in the Sand

The reluctance to put away childish things may be a requirement of genius.

Rebecca Pepper Sinkler

A sense of adventure is never as prevalent as it is when you are a child. When my twins, Sydney and Lincoln, were three, my husband and I took them on a two-week sailing vacation to visit their Grandma and Papa, my parents, who spend their winters on their thirty-eight-foot sailboat in the British Virgin Islands. My Auntie Carol Ann and Uncle Ken also joined us for part of this journey in their own sailboat, completing our little flotilla.

Our holiday was filled with sailing adventures and countless trips to beautiful beaches to let the kids run off some energy. Over the course of the holiday, Uncle Ken and Papa would entertain the children with tales of the swashbuckling pirates from the past. They filled their heads with visions of sunken ships and buried treasure. Pirates dominated our trip. Sydney learned how to say "ARGH!" while at the helm of the boat. Lincoln pointed out Jolly Roger flags that decorated other boats, saying,

"Pirates, Papa! Look! There's pirates!" And Grandma outfitted them with plastic hooks and eye patches after a trip to a souvenir shop. The whole idea of pirates, with their tall ships and hidden chests of treasure, was fascinating to Sydney and Lincoln, and on almost every beach that we visited, one of them would inevitably ask, "Do you think there is pirate treasure on this beach?"

Two days before we were ready to leave, we dropped anchor in a gorgeous little bay with one of the most beautiful white sandy beaches we had seen yet. The kids were anxious to get to shore to explore this new beach and find some pretty shells to add to their collection. We piled into the dinghy and made the journey to land, where Auntie Carol Ann and Uncle Ken came rushing over to greet us.

"Kids, look what we found!" exclaimed Auntie Carol Ann. "A treasure map. It must have been left by pirates!"

And sure enough, in her hands was a beat-up piece of paper with some scratched-up markings that must be directions to the hidden treasure.

Sydney and Lincoln's jaws dropped. They couldn't believe their luck! A pirate map and they had it! The kids grabbed up the map and began their adventure (with a little help from Mom). The map started at the rocky boulders that bordered the beach; from there, they took three big steps until they found three sticks laying in a row. The sticks pointed them in the direction they were to walk until they found a circle of stones. They consulted their map, looking for the next clue. As they made their way through the clues on the map, more and more sunbathers left their towels on the sand and wandered over to see what they were doing, and soon a small crowd had grown to see what was going on. After a few more maneuvers, they found what they had been searching for, the "X" that marked the spot.

The frantic digging began, with sand flying in every

direction. After only a few seconds, the beautiful white sand reveled its secret, the pirate's treasure chest that they had been hearing about for the last two weeks, and their small audience cheered. They couldn't believe their luck as they pulled out a little treasure chest that had been thoughtfully buried in a Ziploc bag to keep the sand out. They lifted the lid and revealed their loot. *Wow!* These pirates must have had kids; their treasure consisted of candy, toy cars, and pretty bracelets.

My children talked about their pirate treasure on the beach for weeks afterward, and for months they would show off their "loot" to anyone who would listen. There may have been toys and candy in that little toy chest, but for anyone who was on the beach that day, we all know that the real treasure wasn't in the chest buried in the sand.

Elena Aitken

Family Cottage

The family cottage—it has a nice ring to it, doesn't it?

It suggests a place where the warm closeness of the clan outshines the summer's sun on even the cloudiest of days; a place where the relatives gather to bask in the glow of togetherness; a place to communally "break bread," even if it is at a kitchen table that only seats four. And a retreat where the extended family can all sleep under the same roof.

Yes, perhaps it's on sofas and in sleeping bags on the living room floor because there are only two bedrooms in the whole cottage, but this is the lake! So what if you're forced to share a bathroom the size of a phone booth with nine other people, three of whom are children clammering, "I have to go potty; I HAVE TO GO NOW, MOMMY." You'll just have to forget your usual twenty-minute "sit-down" and perusal of the sports page; that will have to wait until you get back to the city.

When my in-laws bought the cottage at Winnipeg Beach sixteen years ago, it was with the hope that every summer from that day on, the entire Melnicer family, en masse, would head out there on the long Victoria Day weekend and remain there to collectively laze and play and upgrade until Labour Day arrived. This marked the time when we would officially close down the cottage for the season (which is Winnipeg Beach vernacular for "having Cain, the plumber, turn the water off"). It was the Southfork concept of cottage life that my husband's parents embraced. Perhaps they'd seen too many episodes of *Dallas* (my theory, but then I'm an only child); perhaps it was the model based on their own Eastern European families, large, loving, and boisterous, happily dwelling together in close quarters. Whatever the reason, the plan was clear. For more than three months every summer we would all live together in harmony and love, cooperating and compromising blissfully, day after sun-kissed day.

Seated on the porch at the end of another perfect day, we'd watch the sun set over the lake. And we would do this in less than seven hundred square feet of space, counting the porch, for three months, with one minuscule bathroom—forgive me, I'm repeating myself.

Now here's the unbelievable part. I actually bought into this insanity, at least for a short time. Why did I go along with this craziness, you ask? For the sake of the family, of course!

We were going to live like the Waltons. As an only child, I dreamed of being a Walton! The fantasy went like this: at bedtime, like John-Boy, we'd say good-night to everyone else in the house, calling out sweetly to one another from room to room; then, in the morning, we'd discuss our plans for the day over a wholesome, delicious breakfast like the Nelsons, and in the evening, like Princess tripping down the Andersons' stairs at the end of a busy day, we'd exuberantly share all of the exciting events that made up the past eight hours. I was going to live the dream. "Sharon-Girl" couldn't wait.

I'm not sure exactly when it all began to unravel. I think it might have been the snoring.

Of course, I had heard my husband snore before. In fact, his snoring was so loud some nights that I had to escape his heaving, chain-saw rumbles by exiting our bedroom altogether and utilizing my second line of defense, industrial-strength, gel earplugs. At the cottage, I learned for the first time that my husband's snoring was part of his rich, genetic legacy, and that, unlike the Three Tenors, there was nothing soothingly operatic about this Melnicer threesome in concert.

Finding an alternative place to sleep was a challenge. The living room, by that time of night, was fully occupied, and we were definitely out of bedrooms. So I spent the first of many nights camped out in the mosquito-infested backseat of our "spacious" two-door Plymouth Horizon.

The waiting-in-line for a turn in the bathroom was another contributor to my coming undone. Urgency often forced me to head for the nearest dogwood bush in the overgrown backyard; brushing my teeth with the power-nozzle end of the hose got to be commonplace. But I think, in retrospect, the lack of privacy was the thing that completely sent me over the top.

No action or behavior went unobserved. Itches in private places had to go unscratched; flatulence had to be quietly contained. A normal sex life was becoming a thing of the past; I even began to hate all children. In short, life in the fishbowl was beginning to wear thin.

My husband, forever the optimist, continued to nurse the dream of the "family cottage" for a few more summers. In fact, at one point, to placate me and to show me he was sensitive to my needs, he suggested that we renovate the wooden storage shed out back (not far from my favorite bush) and make it into our own "private little cottage." "Little" is right! It was smaller than the bathroom! And it would have cost $8,000 to fix up!

Thankfully, sanity prevailed. I think it was the estimate

for renovating the shed that finally sunk in. I decided that I would be happier spending summer in the city, and that I'd go out to the lake occasionally for the day, sometimes even for the night.

My daughter usually went with my husband, but she knew that she had the option of remaining at home with me, too. Joint cottage custody, if you will.

For a while I bore the guilt of being the dream breaker, you know, the one who had to rain on the parade. There were some strained silences, some awkward conversations, but gradually, the idea of "Southfork" receded and respect for individual needs received some well-deserved attention. But what's most important is that I got my twenty-minute sit-down with the sports section back. And we all got to be a happy family again.

Sharon Melnicer

Not My Idea of the Hilton

Every survival kit should include a sense of humor.

Author Unknown

Some of my husband's fondest memories from his childhood revolved around his summers at Lake Winnipesaukee in New Hampshire. He was determined to share that with his children. So like a dutiful wife, I packed up the kids and off we went.

My introduction to Sandy Island was not auspicious. The family camp operated by the Greater Boston YMCA was on a rustic island in the middle of Lake Winnipesaukee accessible only by motorboat. It was pouring rain when Paul loaded his wife, two children, diapers, and mother-in-law onto the launch and blissfully went off to sail his Sunfish over to the island.

Packed into a tarpaulin-covered retired Coast Guard launch with all the other "campers," my two small children and my mother were drenched and cold as we made our way across the lake. Sullen teenage camp counselors assisted us onto a slippery dock. Fellow campers scattered quickly for shelter from the driving rain. Mom and I followed stupidly, having no idea where else to go. We made our way to a lone light shining a few feet into the woods.

A cheerful woman greeted us when it was our turn and handed me a map to our cabin. Off we went into the woods to find our cabin. I pushed the umbrella stroller with a very hefty nine-month-old John while Mom took Robyn by the hand, both of us overburdened with our totes. The kids were hungry, soaking wet, and whining, but they were in a much better mood than their mother.

All of a sudden, Mom came to a complete stop, her feet ankle-deep in the mud. I almost crashed into her with the stroller.

She looked at me with tired, rheumy eyes, dripping white hair, her favorite sweater drenched and muddy, and quietly said, "I lost my shoe."

Mom's shoes weren't exactly shoes. They were just a step up from slippers. She wasn't stylish but she was comfortable. However, now she was barefoot. We rummaged around in the mud. No shoe.

Mom and I trudged along some more. Then it was my turn to let out a wail as the stroller, with my baby boy, encountered the deep root of a massive oak tree obscured by three inches of mud. The flimsy aluminum of my Kmart special crumbled, and John, still tethered to the canvas seat, landed face first in soggy pine needles.

That was it. I yanked his poor cherubic face out of the mud, his tears mingling with mine as we both sank under that huge oak, sobbing. Mom looked on helplessly with Robyn placidly by her side.

I heard my husband's voice call my name, but it took me a moment to locate him standing on the porch of a rough-hewn cabin. I started yelling between sobbing. What I was yelling can't be repeated here.

Somewhat chagrined, he came off his dry perch to assist

his very distraught wife and drenched family onto the porch and into a dry cabin.

"What do you think?" He spread his arms wide to take in the bare cabin, smelly mattresses, and moldy pillows.

He asked so I told him, completely shattering his enthusiasm. Mom stood a few feet away. That was about as far as she could get from this domestic squabble in the tight confines of this rustic gem.

There is no way to describe my disappointment and horror at the thought of being stuck in this drafty cabin on this drowning lake with my barefoot mother, two crying toddlers, and my inconsiderate husband (after all, how could he bring me to such a place?). I was stuck here for a week. You came on a boat on Saturday, and you left on a boat the next Saturday. Our luggage was being delivered by some anonymous boat people, so we were stuck in wet clothes.

My daughter announced she had to go to the bathroom.

"You have to hike up that path into the woods. It's a communal bathroom and shower," Paul informed me. Quickly realizing this was not good, he added, "I'll take her."

So much for spending seven days on the beach soaking up the sun. So far all I had managed to soak up was half of Lake Winnepausaukee.

The rain lasted for three days. The sun came out. We still trudged through the mud wherever we had to go. It takes forever for mud to dry under all the towering pine trees. Paul very patiently coaxed me out of my mood. He has a talent for doing that. Mom carried on like a trouper. The kids had activities to do during the morning. Mom watched them during naptime. Paul introduced me to sailing; I think it's the thing he loves most in the world after the kids and me.

On Thursday, Doc Anderson approached our table at

dinner. He presented my mother with a soggy, muddy mass that vaguely resembled her lost shoe.

Friday was water carnival day with canoe competitions and games for the kids and adults. Paul, twenty-eight years old, revisited his childhood in the games. He joined the men in all the competitions and canoe wars. He took his stint on the log and water wrestled his way to King of the Log.

Friday night was show night. All the little kids paraded out on the stage to show off the skits they had learned at camp. Amateur adult performers regaled us with bad jokes and even worse singing. The evening ended with the camp song. My tone-deaf husband sang at the top of his lungs, joined by his daughter who had learned the song at camp.

Saturday morning dawned bright and sunny as we boarded the launch back to the mainland. Mom and I boarded the launch, Paul with us this time. He wisely decided he might sail the boat over early and return to render assistance to his wife and mother-in-law.

As the boat pulled away from the dock, he said, "So, what do you think?"

I looked at my husband, tears rolling down my cheeks.

"That bad?" he asked.

"That good!" I kissed him. "Can we come back next year?"

When the sun came out, Sandy Island was as magical as my husband had described to me all these years. We returned to Sandy year after year, for another sixteen years.

Bonnie Walsh Davidson

"Remind me to send an e-mail to the Weather Channel
saying 'Wrong again!' Will you?"

Reprinted by permission of Stephanie Piro. ©2004 Stephanie Piro.

Caught on Video

Many people who are not from the east coast of Canada assume that it is too cold here most of the time to enjoy many beach days. After all, the area I'm speaking of, located in the middle of the North Atlantic, has birthed tales of giant icebergs that sink ships, autumn gales that terrify, and snow that at times reaches the tops of the telephone poles. Although these tales are all true, Cape Breton Island, just east of Nova Scotia, has also spawned tales of beautiful days spent on sandy beaches that stretch for miles and miles, with such unique and warm ocean currents that pass through this area, you would think you were in your bathtub. I have one such memorable tale that ended in something I will never forget, and which I will cherish forever.

The day started like any other July or August day on the cape. My parents packed up the van with lunches, towels, and beach gear, while my sisters and I gathered our favorite beach toys to add to the already crowded van. We pack a lot, but you have to understand what a day on the beach here entails. It's a big event that begins early in the morning and goes well into the night, next to a warm fire. After all, East Coast winters are very long and hard, so we have to get as much sun as possible before going back into hibernation.

It takes about an hour to drive to our favorite beach, which is located at the mouth of the famed Mira River. This particular day, we arrived a bit later than normal and were unable to stake out our usual place on the beach as it was already taken by another family. We were somewhat upset by this, but soon found a suitable place to set up camp for the day. We spent the day swimming and making sand castles, only taking a break to eat dinner.

It was close to the end of our meal when I noticed some people getting out of a big white van. I noticed them because they didn't look like typical beachgoers, as they were wearing jeans and T-shirts. What gave them away even more was all the equipment they were carrying down to the beach. From where I was, it looked like camera equipment. I was then distracted by the activity around me and quickly forgot the commotion unfolding down the beach.

Soon after we finished our meal, we packed up all the gear and headed back down the beach to our van. We were oblivious to the men unloading the camera equipment onto the beach until one of them started toward us. After he had a short conversation with my dad, us kids were ushered toward an area next to the bridge where we were given instructions to sit around the fire, roast marshmallows, look like we're having fun, and smile a lot. We were going to appear in a music video.

We rehearsed a couple of times, and when we were ready, the cameras started rolling. After only a couple of takes, it was all done and we were relieved from our duties and given five dollars each for our time. That five-dollar bill was spent rather quickly on a trip to the Bayside canteen for ice cream on the way home. But I didn't realize how priceless the experience was until the night arrived when the music video, "Song for the Mira" performed by Anne Murray, was broadcast on CBC across the nation. The song itself is a masterpiece, and the video couldn't have depicted the magic of the Mira River any better. And there we were, around the campfire playing our part like the cameras were not even rolling. A memorable day on the banks of the Mira River caught on video to enjoy forever and share with all of Canada!

Andrea MacEachern

Frozen Dreams

Never a ship sails out of the bay but carries my heart as a stowaway.

Roselle Mercier Montgomery

After putting the hot chocolate packages, marshmallows, cookstove, and matches in a knapsack, we piled on our winter clothes and skied to the beach. The sun had finally come out, and we felt like explorers at the North Pole, though we were only in Michigan, cross-country skiing through the woods and leaving only our tracks on the fresh snow. Looking at the empty cottages, we imagined what it'd be like living in one of them surrounded by the snow-covered trees, away from parents, brothers, and sisters.

Both Linda and I wished we could swap homes. She wanted to live within walking distance of the library, and I longed to live near the beach. But on this wintry day, the best homes were these deserted cottages.

"I'd live in this cottage all year if I owned it," I said, nodding to an old three-story house.

"Maybe we'll be famous writers when we're older, and one of these big cottages will be ours."

"You think we'll ever be rich, Linda?"

"I will be."

We skied on in silence, both lost in our private thoughts until reaching a clearing overlooking the lake. "It's beautiful!" I screamed. Ten-foot waves had been frozen solid, just as they were breaking against the shore. There was nothing but icebergs for miles up and down the shore.

"My dad's fishing boat is stuck out there," Linda said, pointing at Lake Michigan. "It happens every winter."

"When do you think he'll be back?"

"When the ice melts. Unless the Coast Guard finds a way to haul them to shore in Racine, they won't be coming back to Holland for awhile."

My dad worked at a factory during the day. He punched in, punched out, and came home grumpy, while Linda's dad and his fishermen friends hung out in the fish shed telling jokes and talking about their wild adventures. During the warm months, I'd ride my bike to her house on Sundays so I could drink a Dr. Pepper with the men, hoping I'd be invited to go out on the fishing boat.

"They like fishing to get away from their wives," Linda said. "Even I don't get to go out with them. It's a guy thing."

"Wouldn't it be fun if we had an all-girl fishing boat?"

"I don't want to fish. I'd rather work in a factory."

We skied down the dune to the beach. Everything looked so foreign. It seemed like the people climbing the dunes could have been explorers on Mars. We propped our skis in the snow and joined the others walking on the frozen ice, but walking just a little further out than the rest. We were certain this thick ice wouldn't break.

"Here's a good spot out of the wind," Linda decided.

The sun was starting to set while we heated water in a pan. Both of us kept our hands over the flame, thawing out our fingers while the temperature dropped with the disappearing sun.

"One of these days I'm going to walk around the entire lake, Linda."

"Why?"

"Just to do it. I want to see the people who live in northern Michigan and Wisconsin."

"There are channels you'd have to get across, just like the one over there by the lighthouse."

"I could swim them."

"Maybe. I'd rather move to France for an adventure."

"That seems so far away."

"That's why," Linda laughed. She was one year older and seemed to know way more than me. It would take me awhile to find France on the map hanging on Linda's bedroom wall, but she could point out any river or country without thinking about it.

Sitting on the iceberg, we drank our hot chocolate watching the people leave the beach, wondering where we'd live, which places we'd visit, and what famous books we'd write.

Before skiing home, we looked for Linda's dad's fishing boat, but saw nothing except frozen water blending into the gray sky—nothing but icebergs, nothing but dreams.

Diane Payne

The Beach Club

As far back as I can recall, my family and I spent our summers at our cabana at Silver Point Beach Club on Long Island, New York. The memories we made at the beach are among the fondest memories I have. My father had passed away the summer before I turned four, and when I think of my dad, I can see him in our cabana or out on the sand or splashing in the water, just enjoying the lazy summer days. I wish he could have enjoyed more summers with us, but at least he'll always be at the beach in my mind.

Three carloads of us would arrive at the beach very early in the morning: my mom, my two sisters, my brother, my aunt and uncle, my two cousins, and any guests we'd invited to join us that day. We'd march down the boardwalk in single file, our arms heavy with bags of food, supplies, clean towels, clothes, and whatever else we thought we might need.

We'd quickly unpack so we could sit down to eat breakast. Our days basically revolved around mealtimes. We'd begin the morning with warm bagels and an assortment of spreads. Then we'd all part for a few hours to build sand castles, play paddle ball, swim, read, or search out new and old friends. Then we'd be be back for lunch:

cold cuts and rye bread and an assortment of salads and soda.

Harry and Henrietta—who seemed very old to me at five, but were probably only in their mid-thirties—had the big corner cabana at the end of our row. They'd give us kids chocolate-covered graham crackers whenever we passed by. I was a chubby kid and cookies were usually withheld, but Harry and Henrietta always had one for me. I'd pass by their cabana as many times a day as I could come up with reasons.

After lunch, we'd find creative ways to have fun. We'd carve airplanes and cars out of the sand, using whatever we could find to create seats, wings, and controls. We'd spend hours creating these masterpieces that took only minutes to crush and fill. We also made easy things from the sand and water, like cakes, pies, and cupcakes. Then we'd sell them to the adults for a penny each. We'd take these treasured pennies down the boardwalk, looking for things to buy from the kids who had their wares (painted shells and sea glass) set up on their superhero towels. We'd get to pass Henrietta's cabana for another cookie— both ways.

Sometime after lunch, we'd usually go to the pool. There were two pools—the "big" pool and the kiddie pool. I never bothered with the kiddie pool. I just jumped into the deep end of the big pool one day and never came out. I loved swimming and even participated in the annual swimming races every summer. The pool was great, but I loved the ocean too. I'd jump the waves and dive headfirst into them alongside my uncle. Then we'd trudge across the large expanse of sand back to the cabana to shower off the salt water—just in time for dinner.

My mom and aunt would be busy in the small cabana, making us what seemed like a feast after such an active day. We'd sit around the table—the adults at theirs and the kids at ours—and we'd talk about the day and what we would do the next day.

We'd all hang around for a while after dinner, then we kids would change into our PJs for the ride over the bridge. It was okay to be going home; we knew we'd be back the next day—even if it was raining. The rain couldn't keep us away. We had such fun huddling inside the cabana wrapped in our towels and oversized sweat-shirts and telling spooky stories, playing cards, reading, or, of course, eating. We were all so close then, and I couldn't imagine that days like these would someday come to an end.

When we were a bit older, my cousin and I would pull a pair of chairs down to the water's edge and sit and talk about anything and nothing. We'd share our fears, hopes, wonders, and dreams. We'd talk about the "old" beach-club days when we used to play team tag in the place we called the "zoo"—rows and rows of lockers for people who didn't have cabanas.

I experienced many "firsts" at the beach club: my first job (as the arts and crafts counselor at the beach club camp), my first crush (on our cabana boy), and even my first kiss. I'd made so, so many memories at the beach, but I always knew there were more to come, more summers ahead. Even when we kids were all grown up, we'd meet at the beach on the weekends. My niece and I would climb the lifeguard chair and watch the sunset together while I'd tell her of all the cool things I used to do at the beach. When I got married, my husband made himself busy repairing the cabana, which had seen much wear and tear in the course of thirty years.

Although the cabana was still in the family, at some point we stopped being there as a family. All too soon, it seemed, we went our separate ways, and my husband and I found ourselves living across the country. Finally, my mom and aunt decided to let the cabana go, to let another family have it, to create their own cherished memories of growing up on the beach.

I haven't been back to Silver Point since we moved out west, but I can always visit it in my mind. I vacation at the beach—any beach—as often as possible. I drop my things in my hotel room, and then practically run down to the water. I make a sand trail with my feet, swooshing the hot sand back and forth until I reach the cool, wetter sand. I still anticipate a good rainstorm and the card game that's sure to follow, along with the chocolate-covered graham crackers I'll buy in the hotel lobby.

When I close my eyes and concentrate, I can see, hear, feel, and taste the Silver Point Beach Club. I imagine looking out onto the ocean from the railing of the stilts. I see the seagulls zigzagging over the garbage cans. I see the heavy green doors of the cabana. I look where the sand ends and the water starts. I see the umbrellas and chairs. I hear the waves crashing and people laughing. I smell the salt in the air and feel it on my skin. I feel almost four again, dragging my feet through the sand to leave my trail, twisting my body back and forth, and thinking of how good it feels to be part of a family, how good it feels to be loved.

Karen Falk

A Seacliff Serenade

Love must be as much a light as it is a flame.

Henry David Thoreau

He was fifteen, or so he lied. I was fifteen (the truth). And the night I met thirteen-year-old Michael B. around a driftwood fire on Seacliff Beach was immense: it meant I was no longer romantically backward. Finally, like all my junior high school friends had already, it was my turn to fall in love for the first time, and Michael flipped me into the abyss with his eyes of Aegean Sea blue and manner as shy as mine.

That was thirty-five years ago.

Today, the details of my first romance, the magic of my first love, live in my mind and heart as a seaside serendipity of sun, sand, surf, and stars. Seacliff Beach is where my first boyfriend and I swam and splashed and laughed: my first kiss, my first beer, my first French kiss—all with Michael B.—all at Seacliff Beach.

Now, a lifetime later, I suspect the beach is bewitched. I mean, really, what can Seacliff be thinking? This California crescent of shore where dolphins frolic, seabirds play, and

sun and stars smile down on a beautiful central coast—
well, it seems the beach is bringing back to me the love I
knew at fifteen. And it is not simply the flush of thrill, the
rush of something new, unexpected, or immense. It is, as
well, the boy himself, his Aegean Sea eyes unchanged in
all this time.

Not that he washed up with the tide, although he might
have for all my surprise. But just last week as I walked the
beach, there he was: my first love, running along the sand.
And to see him, these thirty-five years worth of ex-
boyfriends later, is to realize with an uncomfortable start,
I hardly have evolved at all!

I confess, not since my teenage romance have I managed to swim and splash and laugh in the ocean surf with
the same free and easy abandon that ran like the wind
through the me of fifteen. And let's be honest: In my three
and a half decades of travel to other beaches on a handful
of continents, not a single one has offered so much as a
harmless flirtation, much less an enjoyable fling, far less a
serious love.

But the beach that is the site of my teenage triumph,
where I fell in love during a sunburned summer of surfing
and swimming and fun—I think it is up to something.

Michael is newly divorced (the truth). At age fifty-one, I
am starting over. That's a lie. At age fifty-one-and-a-half
and fresh from a long romance gone wrong, I, too, am
beginning again. So, tripping upon my first love at this
precise moment in time on the very sand where magic
once upon a time whirled me in a dance of freshly awakened desire, a dance that tossed me up, up into the realm
where all feels possible—well, it does seem slightly suspect. Early this evening I walked to the beach from the
family house to which after years away I have returned,
unsure of where the life I play out next will be—this city
or that? In silence I converse with the very same sun,

sand, and sea that long ago held so much promise for the clueless me of fifteen. "Come now, Seacliff, out with it," I say. "Is bringing me Michael your sly, wily way of match-making—again?" The surf speaks not; the birds keep mum.

Returning to Seacliff now, what feels like a lifetime later, I find its enchantment remains—made all the more daz-zling by my travels. No sands of San Sebastian or Cannes seem as clean, no bay of L.A. or Maine or Spain so unique. Mornings when the porpoises leap and evenings when the pelicans feed, I feel there is no better beach in the world for revealing how greatly I'm blessed—blessed not only to revel again in the outdoor joy that is Seacliff's gift to all who love a beautiful beach, but blessed also by this: the far-fetched idea—dare I name it hope?—that the place may have plans for me, plans for something beyond my dreams to which, given my iffy romantic history, I would typically think, *No way!*

Mystery—tales of true love are thick with it. Dashed dreams, apparent loss, and then, at the bleakest eleventh hour, a happy—even miraculous—reconciliation. It is all so sappy, granted, but oh-so-thrillingly romantic! The story is a truth (or lie) I like. So I ask the all-seeing stars that with the faintest sparkle bid sweet dreams to the retiring sun, what is up with me and my first love? The winking firmament says less than Seacliff itself, though I admit the beach is taunting me with hints of what may be for Michael and me. On any day this is what I see: laugh-ing couples hand in hand who stroll the beach at sunset; walkers and their romping dogs who frolic in the surf at dawn. Sunbathers, swimmers, fishers—the beach by light is peopled by the relaxed, the happy, the smiling. By night the otters and sea lions and, when the month is right, whales, add to the sea their wonder. Looks to me like a lovefest, all right. Hmm.

It would be a lie to say the togetherness that Michael and I share again is not an exact replay of our high school relationship. Never mind the thirty-five-year absence. When I splash and laugh and swim with—and kiss—the teenage boy who, at forty-nine, seems strangely unchanged, no time has passed. He's more worldly, perhaps, more traveled; that he has his driver's license now only adds to all the appeal he held for me at thirteen. The truth: Even decades lived apart, often at opposite ends of the earth (me: Paris; Michael: New Zealand) compact into minutes when the free, easy fun once shared with someone again turns up—undiluted, undiminished, undimmed—weird. Or is it a trick of the miraculous? My dear Seacliff, do tell! In my silent conversation, I ask the beach to tell its secret. But the still-warm sand stays silent and the prancing surf rolls in—without a word.

When Michael joins me we build a driftwood fire, he and I, and talk of nothing. We say simply everything in the fun it is to be at this beach after thirty-five years of—whatever, together. We look over the water to the lights of a far-away pier. Suddenly—and this is the truth—porpoises leap from the water, one and then another. Sandpipers scurry, pelicans swoop, and from off somewhere a mockingbird sings. The beach rolls in ecstasy around us, and at a strangely synchronized time, from points practically a planet apart (me: San Francisco; Michael: Indonesia), my first love and I each are drawn back to the same crescent of sea where a love that was new and young arrived once before. Could this be a love not done with us? It is only the beach that knows.

The sky streaks a palette of pinks as the sun sinks behind the horizon. The fog rushes in as if late for a date with destiny. It seems as eager to get back to this beach as weeks ago I was—Michael, too—each of us having felt some mysterious pull neither he, nor I, can explain. Snug by our driftwood fire, my first love and I revel in the moment—repeated. You rascal, Seacliff: the beach where magic happens.

Colette O'Connor

Sands of Time

*Memory . . . is the diary that we all carry about
with us.*

Oscar Wilde

Four hundred years ago, my ancestor Robert Cushman climbed out of a small craft called the *Mayflower* and stepped onto the shore of Massachusetts for the first time. And for almost one hundred years, with only a few lapses, my extended clan has returned to gather for family reunions each summer on those shores of Cape Cod. In the early 1900s, my parents took a train to the remote reaches of the cape. By the time my cousins and I came along, we traveled by car along paved roads.

Every family album contains photos of multiple generations of Robert's descendants playing in the waves and building castles in the sand. Stories, too, have collected over the decades, and I've noticed some stories have gained a momentum of their own as they tumbled from generation to generation.

I remember playing with my Uncle Hervey's children on the beach, enjoying the sun and listening to the waves wash the shore. One day when lunchtime drew near, my uncle asked his youngest daughter, Polly, to run back to the cottage and make sandwiches for the family. Sure enough, twenty minutes later, twelve-year-old Polly emerged carrying a tray of sandwiches. As everyone reached out for them, Hervey asked what type of sandwiches she had made.

"Peanut butter with bologna on raisin bread," she replied.

Abruptly, hands withdrew from the tray and Hervey asked, "What made you choose that combination?"

"Because if you make good sandwiches, everyone eats them too fast," Polly answered.

Most of her brothers and sisters found excuses that day to hike back to the cottage to make their own lunches.

Preparing meals at the beach was always a challenge, given the meager facilities in the rented cottages. Nevertheless, all of us continued to thrive in the fresh air and freedom of the holiday atmosphere. Year after year, we collected driftwood (as Uncle Leslie would say, "Business is picking up on the beach!"). We sunbathed until people warned us about UV rays and skin cancer. We played games of canasta, Monopoly, and Scrabble. We visited favorite landmarks like Highland Light.

And we grew older and taller. After a year apart the big question among the sixteen cousins was, "Who was now the tallest?"

My brother Robert (yes, named for our long-ago ancestor) and his cousin young Hervey stood back to back in the living room of the cottage.

"No fair, you're standing on the carpet while I'm on the linoleum."

Today we are still growing older, but no one even cares who is the tallest. Instead we watch our own children at play and recall memories of our youth. And I like to think of our ancestor Robert looking down and watching as each new generation begins building its own castles of sand.

Emily Parke Chase

The Souvenir

I remember it as if it were yesterday—my first trip to the ocean. Summers spent with Aunt Orpha and Uncle Don at their home in Pennsylvania were always something to look forward to, but a trip to Atlantic City—that was beyond my wildest dreams!

I had never, ever stayed in a hotel, and this one would be right on the beach. My cousin, Cynthia from Trenton, New Jersey, was going to be my playmate, and as giggly thirteen-year-old girls, we were both excited to see each other, to enjoy the miles of beach along the Atlantic Ocean, and explore the famous Atlantic City boardwalk. The landlocked, sprawling city of Detroit where I lived, with its miles of concrete streets filled with honking traffic, had nothing like this.

"Now, girls," Uncle Don said as he gave us our very own room key, "sleep in as late as you want and when you wake up, just pick up the phone and call for room service." *Room service? Breakfast in bed? Sleep as late as you want with no one telling you it's time to get up?* I thought I was dreaming, or better yet, living in the lap of luxury!

The next morning, Cynthia and I woke with great anticipation. With tummies full after ordering just about everything on the breakfast menu, from pancakes to bacon and eggs, we put on our swimsuits and headed for the beach. I thought I had stepped into a picture postcard. Seagulls soared in the brilliant blue sky, and the sun's rays shimmered on the ocean waves. Wiggling our toes in the sugar-white sand, we looked for where the beach towels were spread as our aunt and uncle waited for us to join them. The ocean beckoned, enticing us farther and farther out until the first crashing wave caught us and I tasted my first gulp of salt water. Squealing with delight, Cynthia and I waited for the next rolling wave, determined to jump even higher to avoid another swallow of the salty sea.

That evening after dinner we strolled down the boardwalk, where I had my first sweet taste of saltwater taffy. Vendor stalls were everywhere, selling souvenirs to take back home. "That box of taffy won't even make it back to your hotel room, girls," Uncle Don teased. "Let's find something you can keep longer than that. How about having an artist draw your picture?" With a piece of charcoal in his hand, the boardwalk artist grinned and began to sketch my likeness. As I sat as still as a statue, I thought, *Is this really happening to me? This has got to be one of the best days of my life!* All day long I had felt like a princess, and this was the crowning touch.

Today, the Atlantic City of yesterday is gone—replaced with high-rise condos and casinos. Yet, whenever I open the tattered box of family photos and mementos where the charcoal sketch is stored, I can smell the salt-air breezes, see the leisurely crowds strolling down the boardwalk, and almost taste the saltwater taffy as I envision it being pulled, cut, and wrapped into those tasty morsels. More than the fun times on the beach and boardwalk, it reminds me of the gift that my aunt and uncle continuously shared—lots of time and attention wrapped in love. "Gee whiz," I can hear myself saying, "You sure know how to make a girl feel special!"

Karen R. Kilby

Summer Fun

Two bags of old, stale hot dog rolls they carted to the sand
With expectations of happy seagulls eating from their
hands.
These chubby hands belonged to kids, ages four and a
great big six,
Who promised their mom and daddy, no water and NO
TRICKS!
And so, they ran down joyfully, skipping, and leaping too,
Hit the beach a-giggling, the four-year-old tumbling a
time or two.
Finally, they seized the moment of tearing moldy hot dog
buns,
And threw them in the air about them, ripping through
each one.
The last they saved to eat themselves and sat, and won-
dered when
Their hungry friends the seagulls would discover, descend
on them.
"Here they come!" she shouted as one gull found the
bready scene,
And then the flock hovered; it was almost like a dream.
Jubilant smiles prevailed as the seagulls ate their fill,

And one brave bird decided to munch from her hand into
  his bill.
A successful feeding frenzy had the kids with hot dog
  rolls.
At the beach you make your own fun,
So much fun for young and old!

Julie Callas

6

INSIGHTS AND LESSONS

For whatever we lose (like a you or a me)
it's always ourselves we find in the sea.

e. e. cummings

Daddy's Love

Daddy loved the ocean. He adored everything about it, from the tangy salt scent to the scratch of fine sand between his toes. The sound of the sea was his siren song, and he nurtured this abiding love both within himself and me.

During high school breaks, Wednesdays were "our day," and we cherished them as a gift. We each accepted through tacit understanding that time and my own inevitable maturity would steal those Wednesdays from us, so we treasured the moments and made as many memories as we could.

One of our favorite Wednesday outings was to drive along the New Hampshire coast, sometimes heading into Massachusetts. In the winter we bundled up and walked on the beach whenever the wind and weather permitted, and many times we returned to the car with cheeks and noses chilled red, glad for the warm air blowing from the vents.

The myriad times we spent at the beach have meshed in my mind like a web of fine silk threads, each different in texture and hue but spun into a fine tapestry of cherished memories. Yet there is one day that stands out from the others, a day when Daddy showed me something of uncommon beauty that illuminated my imagination and settled in my heart for a lifetime.

The weather was warming up. It was no longer winter, but not yet spring, and the arcades and amusements at Salisbury Beach were just beginning to open in preparation for warmer weather. The old wooden roller coaster stood idle, a silent sentinel over sand and surf.

There was yet a nip in the air, so we dressed for comfort. Daddy wore a light jacket and I donned my favorite cardigan, one that reached my thighs and offered big front pockets to warm my hands. We walked along the raised wooden platform that stood on the beach and wandered into the nearest arcade. It was empty, except for the proprietor, and we spent at least an hour there playing Skeeball and trying to best each other at pinball.

Our next stop was a little seafood stand that offered delicious fried clams served in greasy red and white cardboard containers. We found a picnic spot and ate there, admired the occasional boat on the horizon, and enjoyed the play of waves against the shore.

I began to feel the cold but was enjoying the day too much to complain. The gusty wind competed with the ocean breakers for sound dominance, so Daddy and I listened to this odd harmony of air and water, savored our clams, and watched the sea.

"It's raining sunshine," Daddy said, nudging my shoulder with his.

I glanced at him askance. It was sunny, but the temperature bordered on cold because of the wind. What on earth was he talking about?

"Look." Daddy nodded to the sea and smiled. "There are sun drops, millions of sun drops."

I blinked back at the surface of the water and felt the smile light my face when I saw the ocean through his eyes.

He was right. It was raining—it was pouring—sun drops!

The silvery sunlight shone down on the huge expanse of sea, and with each watery swirl and shimmering peak, the reflecting rays created the illusion of sunshine rain.

I watched the diamond-bright sun drops dance on the water, the sight so dazzling it made my eyes tear. I had loved and watched the sea my whole life but never noticed the sun drops until that moment.

Those beach days with my daddy are long gone, absorbed into my personal past. They are treasures to touch and hold close, memories of cherished times with a special man. To have them is a blessing, and yet it seems not nearly enough. Still, I am grateful for those days and all the things he taught me.

I learned that day on the beach that beauty manifests itself in unexpected ways, that what I see and how I see it are largely a matter of perspective, not always reality. I learned that things, and people, too, are so much more than what they seem, that hidden treasures abound, even in things we take for granted, if we illuminate a different view, a different angle.

I love the sea and can't smell it or sense it without thinking of Daddy and our special beach days. I think of him, too, when flashing sun drops dance like diamonds on the water.

And I am struck anew by the beauty of it, each and every time.

Lisa Ricard Claro

Now and Then on the Beach

As I walk along the beach
I pick up shells I like to keep
Without a thought I quickly discard
The broken, old, faded, and scarred
Those with colors bright and perfect form
I take them home to call my own
With great care I polish and clean
And put the shells in a special place, to be admired and
   seen
From my years on the shore, my collection I treasure
I recall those walks, with extraordinary pleasure
And when my days on earth are complete
Eternally I will be on the most beautiful beach
As a shell I will delight in the heavenly sand
I will wait anxiously until I am in my Creator's hand
Life's lessons of joy and happiness, grief, and pain
Have left me old and scarred, broken and gray
The beauty of my youth and faded long since
My life though tough has been quite rich
Now I see coming a most comforting sight
It's my Maker, Creator choosing shells with delight

As I wait for my Creator to come
Shells are being chosen for the heavenly kingdom
All I can do is wait patiently and see
And pray he did not take shelling tips from me.

Paula Gunter-Best

Four Blocks Up

The larger the island of knowledge, the longer the shoreline of wonders.

Ralph W. Sockman

My beach boys have come to my home at the shore for a visit. Grandson Ben is six years old, Jake nine. Both understand that they are coming to a special place and life will change dramatically because they are here. There will be a lot of sitting in rocking chairs, telling stories, not rushing about, and hours at the beach. They wave to me from the porch and their faces glisten with anticipation.

"Is it time to go to the beach?" Ben asks. It doesn't matter if it's summer and the town is filled with tourists, or winter and filled with snow. Ben asks the question anyway. For he knows four blocks up, it's waiting. Like a promise never broken—his friend, the ocean, greets him with another friend: tons of sand. And perhaps even the little-boy friend he met a few months ago, running across the beach. Ben already holds his bucket and shovel. He is ready for another shore adventure.

My grandsons have been beach boys since they were

born. In the warm weather, as soon as we approach the
boardwalk, they take off their socks and shoes for they
realize the beach expects such changes. It also expects
them to sift the sand through their fingers, discover an
important seashell, and in the summer, visit the ocean and
get wet. The ocean refuses to be ignored.

As beach boys, one of Ben and Jake's first lessons is to
learn to respect the ocean. It demands respect. Though it
plays with them, runs up and gently touches their legs,
splashes against their faces tenderly, they realize it has
another side. Young beach boys learn this early in life. So
they must always be at the ocean's edge with an adult
watching them. They must understand from an early age
that the ocean doesn't realize its own energy, and it sometimes can overpower an unsuspecting human being.

When both are on the beach, they are always discovering
new treasures, like the seagulls soaring overhead, cawing
to one another and dipping low over the beach as if to
greet them. Or the foghorns, constant in the distance on a
day when the fog rolls in from the ocean and blankets the
shore. The ocean communicates with my grandsons, and
they have learned to know its moods. On a stormy day it
thunders against the jetties and sounds like a train rushing down the street toward us.

There is much to entertain Ben and Jake when they are
here. Cars, hundreds of them, rush into the town at
summertime with boats, bicycles, and beach chairs
attached. Tourists pack the sidewalks. They are hurrying
to escape. They are getting away from ticking clocks and
schedules and jobs. The ocean will see to it that they forget what they have left behind. "Can we go fishing later?"
Jake asks. His fishing poles are waiting in the shed. He
watches the fishermen walk by, carrying their poles, the
families carrying picnic baskets and blankets and beach
chairs. They are laughing, happy. It is vacation time—

when everybody looks good and feels good—when reality packs its belongings and heads out of town.

"Can we go to the beach, Ga Ga?" one asks after the other. They are already walking toward the boardwalk, as if being pulled in that direction.

In a world that changes from moment to moment, Ben and Jake can count on the beach always guarding the ocean—waiting for them—four blocks up.

Harriet May Savitz

Condo Without a View

The best thing one can do when it's raining is to let it rain.

Henry Wadsworth Longfellow

"Ocean view condo near the beach" read the brochure. I closed my eyes and visualized salty breezes, swaying palms, and warm sand between my toes. Our anniversary falls on March 16, and this year I wanted to celebrate it at the beach. When I informed my husband, Dan, of my idea, he groaned.

"I don't want to spend our anniversary freezing at Myrtle Beach."

"Oh, pooh. Myrtle Beach will be warm by March, and we'll get the cheap rates. Think of those juicy shrimp dinners."

We arrived at Myrtle Beach on a Saturday afternoon—the only occupants in the entire resort. Dan glared at me as we removed our luggage from the trunk. A cold rain stung our faces.

"Now take it easy, Dan. Let's just get to our room and unpack. I'm sure the weather will warm up."

"I hope so. There's no way I'm sitting on the beach when it's only forty-nine degrees."

We unlocked the door to our condo and confirmed that our room had an ocean view, as promised. Only you needed a telescope to see it. We had no problem seeing the dumpster and the asphalt parking lot.

The next day Dan and I donned our bathing suits at my insistence and headed for the beach. We also wore our sweat suits since the weather was still a little chilly. The wooden boardwalk to the ocean resembled the Great Wall of China. It went on and on, over marshland and sand dunes, as we stumbled along its uneven boards, occasionally tripping over nails sticking up through the floor.

Finally, we arrived at the beach, where a brisk wind whistled through the sand dunes. I removed my sweat suit and made a feeble attempt to sunbathe.

"Are you crazy?" asked Dan. "You're not going to get a tan. You're going to get pneumonia."

Five minutes of goose bumps and shivering convinced me that Dan was right. I put my sweat suit back on and suggested a short walk to warm us up. With our jackets tightly zipped and our hands stuffed into our pockets, we marched rapidly down the deserted beach. On the way back, we noticed the tide had risen and formed a shallow pool that now blocked our way. It was too cold to wade barefoot through it, but neither of us wanted to walk all the way around it. We were anxious to return to our warm condo.

"We can jump that little pool, Dan. It's not that wide. Let's give it a try."

With my long legs, I sailed into the air and across the pool with no problem. I landed right on the edge of the water and barely wet my sneakers.

"It's your turn, honey. Come on. You can do it."

Pumping his arms, Dan got a running start and shot

into the air like an arrow. First he went straight up. Then
he came straight down. He landed with a big splash right
in the middle of the pool, knee deep in icy water. His eyes
bulged, his nostrils flared, and his teeth chattered, but he
laughed just as loudly as I did at his misadventure. We
retreated hastily to our condo before he froze completely.

The weather never improved during the week. We sal-
vaged what we could of our vacation and anniversary celebration by visiting the malls and stuffing ourselves
nightly with seafood.

"It could have been worse," I told Dan on the way back
to Oak Ridge.

"How?" he responded. "It rained most of the week, and
the temperature never even reached fifty degrees!"

"It's all a matter of perspective, Dan. Just think—we
could have been hit by a hurricane."

Judy DiGregorio

"We got to thinking—Florida has fish too,
and it's a lot warmer."

Reprinted by permission of Patrick Hardin. ©1998 Patrick Hardin.

Dolphins

Nothing in life is to be feared. It is only to be understood.

Marie Curie

My granddaughter Margaret and I are sitting on the edge of our wharf, feet dangling, while we watch a smiling mammal toss a fish high over its head for the third time. The animal splashes and rolls, and before we know it, my previously bored grandchild and I are in the water, tossing a ball, splashing, and laughing—a lesson in making our own fun learned from a dolphin.

I am not surprised, because I have an idea that dolphins, like dogs, have a special kinship with humans. They manage to bridge a metaphysical gap between terra firma and their own mysterious environment, which makes the connection almost magical.

An hour later, Margaret and I are back on the wharf. The creak of the hammock's chain lulls her to sleep while I watch the gray sheen of dorsal fins arcing through green water, remembering a day like this one when Margaret's mother and aunt were little girls.

Loaded down with towels and drinks and floats, we had made our way down the oyster-shell drive, across the shimmering black ribbon of asphalt road, and onto the expanse of a beach that looks more like sugar than sand. We spread towels close to the gently breaking waves, weighing corners against the breeze with flip-flops and shells. A blue heron stood tall and gazed reverentially out over the water like a tourist enjoying his first glimpse of the Gulf of Mexico. I kept one eye on a magazine, the other on my girls splashing at the water's edge.

The heron's irritated squawk made me look over as he took off, his great wings pumping through soft air. An old man with a very large Confederate flag tattooed across his back walked past with a curt nod, sat in the heron's vacated spot, and lit a cigarette. Almost immediately, a group of four or five teenaged boys appeared from the direction of the road. They had long hair, a loud radio, and intimidating attitudes. They looked at us as if we were poison. The old man shot them an equally unfriendly stare. One of the boys mumbled something as he looked our way, and they all laughed and snickered. The old man flinched, sending a flutter across the sagging battle flag, and glanced nervously at my children and me. The boys' mutterings took on low tones, and with narrowed eyes, one of them turned the radio up. The old man took a deep drag, never taking his eyes off the boys, and pegged the rest of his cigarette into the white foam of a breaking wave.

It had taken only a few minutes to turn the atmosphere of that lovely beach ominous with human fear and distrust. The only ones unaware of it were my little girls, who played happily along the seam of a continent and a gulf. I was preparing to gather them, resisting and complaining, along with all of our paraphernalia, when my older daughter called out, "Look! Look at the dolphins!"

Several of them circled and rolled in the calmer water just beyond the sandbar. They made dolphin noises, which I had never heard before. It was as if they were trying to get our attention.

The old man walked over to my daughters. "Look at them fish," he said. "I believe they're talking to you girls."

"Really?" said the children, and the old man smiled.

The boys turned the radio off and gathered near us at the shoreline now, pointing and smiling, children again themselves, enjoying just being boys.

They laughed with the girls, and answered with a polite "Yes, sir" when the old man asked, "Did you see that?"

Suddenly two of the dolphins shot up into the air, shining and sparkling, like silver rockets against the dazzling blue of our summer sky. We were so overcome at the sheer beauty and power of the spectacle that we all began to clap and cheer, brought together by the joy of nature.

When we left, I gave the boys and the old man our leftover drinks. The boys helped us pack up our things. As we trudged through the powdery sand toward the road, I could hear them talking to the old man.

"You ever see dolphins do that?"

"I seen it once on TV," the old man said, "but never out here."

"Man, that was something. Like they were trying to tell us something, you know?"

"Yeah, wonder what it was."

"Heck if I know. Hey, mister, would you like another drink?"

Margaret P. Cunningham

"This is definitely not your typical beach."

The Ocean's Gift

It was her way when life got too complicated, confusing, and overwhelming: She headed for a day at the ocean. There, she usually found a sense of rejuvenation, if not relaxation. There, she found a sense of perspective, if not understanding. There, a sense of peace, if not hope.

Even though it was the middle of February, the day was one that Lady July would have envied. The vase of the sky held only the bright flower of the sun, and it smiled warmly upon her. She could feel it trying to melt her hurt and pain.

The ocean itself was in a raging mood. Huge, rolling waves, white with fury, constantly came to the soaked shore. They pounded out their beat endlessly. Watching them crest and seeing their spray filtered in the sunlight, it seemed that they, too, were shedding tears. As far as she could see up and down the shore and out to sea, it was the same nonstop battering, weeping, and upheaval. Not unlike how her soul was feeling.

Her prayer that day, as it had been for too long, was for a healing of the hurt, healing of her spirit. And yet, more tears came.

It was later in the day when a walk away from the beach

and up a mountainous cliff gave her a different view. High above the shore, she could still see and hear the waves. They hadn't changed what they were meant to do. They were still coming fast and furiously, wrenching all in their way, depositing the demise of their travels on the soul of the shore. From her vantage point, though, she could see beyond the wall of breakers. There, just behind the turmoil, lay the whole of the ocean, calm as a puddle, smooth as a newborn's cheek, peaceful as a whispered promise.

And, as had happened before, she received a gift from the ocean. This gift washed over her and through her and filled her. Standing where she was and seeing the panoramic view helped her to hang on to the belief that if she could just ride out the waves in her soul, then what's beyond them would bring calm, smoothness, and peace.

Their bounty would be endless. The gift was an ocean of hope.

JoAnn Clark

Turtle Dreams

The goal in life is living in agreement with nature.

Zeno

The old sea turtle slowly meandered her way up from the water and high onto the sand. It was almost dark, and I was the only one left on the beach. It was not unusual, on the southern Atlantic coast, to catch a glimpse of a sea turtle digging her nest and laying her eggs, but this one arrived late in the year. The hot sand baking in the sun, it was a perfect incubator, but soon the sea would start roiling from winter storms, and the sun was already sinking low to the south.

I was an eight-year-old dreamer, keeping my intent watch in the near dark. It was late enough; bedtime for me, but as usual, no one knew where I was. I was forbidden to go by myself on the beach at dusk, but nothing could tear me away from my quiet watch. I was about to take part in a miracle.

As I kept my watch on the beach, it became darker and the light grew dim, but I could still see the ancient creature waddle her way upon the shore. Every time she moved, I would creep closer. Trying desperately not to disturb her, I continued to steal forward, not wanting to miss a thing.

By the time the sea turtle began digging, I was very near. She seemed to dig awfully slow. Turtles on the move can move remarkably fast, but this cow was making slow progress. I crept nearer until I was nearly upon her. What was wrong? Then, I saw that the female sea turtle had only one usable back leg. As she dug, she made lopsided progress. I wondered what to do.

All of a sudden her eye moved, and I thought she looked right at me. I felt an incredible urge to help her. I reached beneath her, and I began to dig under her maimed leg. When the hole was nearly big enough to hold me, she stopped digging, and she began to drop her eggs. I quickly moved back to watch: one, two, three, four—each egg dropped rapidly, like little Ping-Pong balls, with soft, leathery shells. There must have been dozens. Tears came to her eyes and dropped onto the sand.

Not knowing that this was a natural part of the sea turtles' birth cycle, I wondered, as a little girl, why she was crying. Was she hurting? Or was she crying because she knew that her babies would not make it home? Perhaps she knew of the people who would steal her eggs or the sea birds that would snatch her babies before they reached the sea. Perhaps it was a way that God provided, so that this little girl could connect through him, with her. When I saw her tears, it hurt my heart. I felt the tears seep from my eyes and drop to the sand, mingling with hers.

When she was finished laying her eggs, the old sea turtle began to fill the hole. I hastened to help her, and still she allowed my intrusion. Then she wandered back down the beach, into the sea, and she dove beneath the waves. I sat there awhile, pondering over this precious miracle in which I participated.

The next day, bright and early, I was on the beach. The nest was easy to spot, high upon the dune, where the sand is dry and no waves reach. The sand looked disturbed because of the digging, so I set to work to disguise it. I gathered seaweed that littered the beach. I carried dried sand from other parts of the dunes, and I gently covered that sacred spot, making it look as though nothing was there.

Every morning before school, I checked, and every afternoon, I checked again. Temperatures remained constant, and the sun shone every day. Weeks later, as I played on the beach, I saw a great trembling in the sand. I thought crabs had invaded the nest, and I hurried over to save the little ones. Right at my feet I began to see the baby sea turtles scramble their way out of the sand, and they hurried down the beach toward the ocean, totally oblivious of me.

Suddenly, the sky was filled with sea birds that launched themselves upon the little turtles. I began to scream, running around and waving my arms, as I tried to chase the birds away. I finally began to pick up the little turtles, using my sweater as a bag. I managed to save perhaps twenty squirming turtles and toss them beneath the waves. Then I sat on the beach and I cried, because I couldn't save them all.

Joy and horror were over in minutes. My life had changed. Such a small event impressed itself heavily on me. For the first time in my life I understood how fleeting life is. How precious are the moments that we are given, and how costly life is if we neglect those moments.

When life seems to overcome me, I often think of that old turtle cow, spending fifty to a hundred years just doing what God intended for her to do. Those thoughts comfort me, and they remind me that though I am slow and getting older, I can still do my part, faithfully and gently. And when life is too hard for me to continue alone, God will always send someone to lend a helping hand.

I was blessed to play a small part in the life of one creature and in the lives of her babies. I discovered that though nature can be very cruel, God is intimately aware of every need, and he will often send someone, just as he sent me to rescue the babies and carry them safely to their home, beneath the waves.

Jaye Lewis

Pebble Magic

A beach is a necessary destination when you live on an island, a tiny chunk of rock in the middle of nowhere. You always catch yourself squinting toward the horizon, looking for other remote islands out there somewhere, perhaps islands with others sitting on beaches, squinting back at you.

One particular day at the beach, life seemed unfair. I'd lost a dear friend to cancer and just felt like sitting by myself, watching the endless waves. I wasn't there to squint or to swim or to sun or to smile.

A stranger approached me. Judging from the striped umbrella and huge beach bag she was toting around, she was a tourist. She handed me a beach pebble, smiled warmly, and walked away. The whole time, she never uttered so much as a word to me.

I watched her get into a rental car and drive off. Puzzled, I examined the off-white pebble in my hand, so cool to the touch. Perfectly rounded by the wonders of the sea, it had a salty smell. Somehow I felt comforted by the pebble. I looked around at all the pebbles surrounding me and realized I wasn't alone on the island, or the planet, after all.

I decided to keep the meaningful gift. It's now six years

later and I still have it on the kitchen windowsill. It's my constant reminder that angels have placed every single pebble on all the beaches of the world.

We can squint or strain our eyes all we want, but chances are we'll never see one of these elusive characters. Just because we can't see angels doesn't mean they haven't been there!

Beach pebbles are the proof. Who else would go to all the trouble to decorate our beaches with so many pebbles that we could never count them?

Roberta Beach Jacobson

Uncle Hamish and the Beach Donkey

I had a lover's quarrel with the world.

Robert Frost

When I was a young girl in northeast Scotland, our home was invaded every summer by relatives who came to have a vacation by the sea. My cousins Jackie and her brother Iain arrived every June and stayed with us throughout their six-week school holidays. There was only one exception to the welcome visitors, and that was Uncle Hamish.

The only good thing about Hamish was that he was married to my mum's sister Dolly, and she was so much fun. When my cousins and I were alone, we used to talk about Uncle Hamish; we dreaded his stay because he did nothing but complain.

He didn't like the seaside and he certainly didn't like children! He complained that the water was too cold and the sand was so fine it blew everywhere. The sand flies always bit him more than anyone else, and he didn't like us going on the donkey rides, as the poor donkeys must be sick of us kids. We paid a small amount most days to ride a donkey along the sand, and we loved it. Nothing pleased Uncle Hamish; his ice cream always melted and fell on his shoes. That never happened to us; mind you, we never had it long enough to let it melt!

In the 1950s, there were two rows of changing huts or cubicles at the top of the beach. They had wooden roofs and canvas sides and a little wooden bench in each one where you could leave your clothes once you had changed into your swimming costume.

Uncle Hamish was in one of these in the front row, just bending over to fold his jacket, when something cold and wet rubbed itself down the back of his legs. He leaped out in alarm, and we all screamed and laughed as one of the donkeys, which had stuck its head into the cubicle to investigate, ran off.

Uncle Hamish changed his views of the donkeys from then onwards. If one came near him, he would glare as if warning it off and then mutter something under his breath that made Aunt Dolly caution him.

I was ten the year that Mum told us "Uncle Hamish has had a heart attack." We weren't quite sure what that was, but we knew by Mum's reaction that it was something serious. It turned out that Uncle Hamish's heart attack had been mild and that he would be all right. Although we didn't like him much, we realized that he might have died and were glad he was okay.

When it came to summer and Mum said, "Guess what, Uncle Hamish and Auntie Dolly are coming as usual," we all tried to smile. We had thought that with his illness, coming to the seaside would thoroughly irritate him and would not be his best option.

It was when we were playing in the garden that I heard Mum and Aunt Dolly talking. "Well, I said to Hamish, 'You have had a warning. Let's stop saving every penny for a rainy day and take a really good holiday for a change!'"

"So what happened that you came back here?" Mum asked her.

"This is what he wanted. He said there was nowhere else he would rather spend his holidays than here on the beach with the kids!" Aunt Dolly explained.

I heard a kind of surprise in Mum's voice at that but all she said was, "I thought he just put up with it all!"

Aunt Dolly laughed, "Oh that's just Hamish's way; he never admits to enjoying himself. The more he complains, the more fun he seems to have!"

We noticed a change in Uncle Hamish; he was much quieter. He didn't glare warningly at the donkeys; he didn't go on and on about the sand blowing into his tea. It worried us that he wasn't complaining. Uncle Hamish was still ill and not really enjoying himself.

That was when I had the brilliant idea of digging a large hole and covering it with a towel while Uncle Hamish was walking along the beach. When he came back to lie down, he stepped on the towel and went tumbling into the hole yelling blue murder. Aunt Dolly and Mum reassured themselves that he hadn't hurt anything, while he demanded to know who had dug the hole.

I told him it was me, so that he would fall in it and get annoyed and then he could enjoy himself. The three adults just stood there staring at me, and I couldn't understand what was so complicated about my idea!

Little more was said to me about this episode, but by the next day Uncle Hamish was complaining how cold the North Sea was and that the sand flies were biting him as usual. I grinned at him, pleased that at last he was enjoying himself.

Every time I rose to do something, Uncle Hamish gave me the kind of look he used to give the donkeys. That pleased me most of all—they had really annoyed him and so my trick had worked!

Joyce Stark

Lasting Treasure

*To give and then not feel that one has given is
the very best of all ways of giving.*

Max Beerbohm

The ocean tugs at my midwestern soul with the same intensity that the moon pulls the tide. Each summer my husband and I visit the seashore, where I walk endless miles on the beach. I've often asked myself why it is that I cannot motivate myself to walk a mile around the city park or in my own neighborhood. I suppose it is the gifts, the treasures indeed, that the ocean tosses in my path, and—if I'm not fast enough—reclaims with rolling waves. My heart pounds with childish excitement at each discovery.

On our last evening of vacation, my husband and I sat in chairs on a desolate sugary-sand beach at sunset, intent on capturing the sights, sounds, and smells, hoping for something tangible to take home. I wandered into the bubbly surf in quest of the perfect treasure, but rejected one broken shell after another.

Instead, I sat down and opted for a photograph of the perfect sunset. The setting sun silhouetted seagulls and pelicans swooping into billowing waves, but clouds soon obscured the view.

I watched a family in the distance walk into the surf. The parents lifted their toddler to the tops of the rolling waves; she appeared to be walking on water. Her laughter carried on the sea breeze. I trained my camera on them until dusk enveloped the beach. As they walked out of the surf, the little girl squealed when she noticed us. She bounded far ahead of her parents, awkward in her gait, head down and belly pooched out. I continued to keep her in my viewfinder, although I could not see features. She ran right toward us, her beach shoes slapping the wet sand, then she plopped her face in my lap and hugged my legs.

Her parents ran swiftly, apologizing for the intrusion.

"Not at all," I said. "I've been looking for a treasure to capture the end of our vacation, and your little girl is just perfect." I stroked her hair.

The toddler giggled, raised her head, and looked into my eyes. At that very moment I learned a lesson about perfection. A crown of wet, glistening, blond curls christened Kaleigh's broad flat face.

Her crystal-blue eyes slanted and protruded, and her oversized, thick tongue fell awkwardly from her mouth.

"Down syndrome children are so lovable and overly friendly with strangers. We're worried it will be a problem. I'm sorry if she got your camera wet," her mom said. She explained that it was also their last day of vacation, and they had been praying for guidance as they frolicked in the ocean. This couple had to make a difficult decision the next day: whether to enroll Kaleigh in a self-contained classroom with special-needs children, or place her in a classroom with normally developing children. They did not know what to do.

Kaleigh babbled, squealed, and chased shore birds as

we conversed. When she hovered too close to me, I stroked her hair and she cooed like the gulls. Her parents apologized repeatedly.

"You must focus on her capabilities, not her disability. Each of us is endowed with special gifts, and your little girl's is friendliness. Don't apologize for her. Accept it; the world needs more friendliness."

"Do you really think so? You're just being nice." Her mom seemed self-conscious. I told her parents that it was no coincidence that we happened upon one another on an isolated beach. "I am a preschool teacher with over twenty-five years experience.

"Inclusion has benefited many of my students, some with autism, behavior disorders, and a variety of learning abilities. The normally developing children come to understand each person's profound uniqueness. And it helps the special-needs children feel a part of the group." We talked until the full moon spotlighted us.

"Thank you so much," her mother said. "You have been a godsend."

In my scrapbook of mementos, I have a photograph of a little girl who taught me a more valuable refresher lesson than any I have ever taught. In my quest for perfection, I was reminded: every seashell, no matter how pitted and broken; every sunset hidden by clouds; every person, regardless of physical or mental condition, is uniquely endowed by our Creator. I believe God sent his little angel to me—as a gift and reminder of his unconditional love. That summer vacation stood out as my most memorable; the treasures I took home were not as tangible as a jar full of seashells, but they will remain long after the seashells are forgotten.

Linda O'Connell

A Flash of Green

Adopt the pace of nature: her secret is patience.

Ralph Waldo Emerson

The sun sets, painting the dusky sky pink, red, and violet. Just as the sun slips below the horizon, its yellow glow yields to a brilliant flash of green.

Thirty years ago I read a magazine article about just such a scene. The author described this green flash as a rare occurrence seen at sunrise on the East Coast and at sunset in the West. It sounded spectacular, and I longed to see it with my own eyes.

That summer our family vacationed at a small resort on the Washington shore. At the close of a cloudless day, I settled on the sand to wait for sunset. I was determined to catch a glimpse of the elusive green flash. Staring into the sinking sun for what seemed like hours, I saw spots of yellow and red behind my eyelids but not a hint of green in the sky. My husband and children lost interest and wandered away, returning now and then to joke about my obsession.

As the last rays of daylight disappeared, the sky turned

black. The sun had set before my bleary eyes without turning green, not even for an instant. My desire unrewarded, I returned to our cabin to face the jibes of my amused family. After that, every trip to the beach gave them the opportunity to tease me about the green flash. "While you're out there, Mom," said my son, "why don't you see if you can spot Bigfoot or the Loch Ness monster?"

"Yeah," my daughter chimed in, "maybe you'll see a UFO!"

My husband, not to be outdone, would add, "Maybe they'll even beam you up!"

Despite their ridicule, I continued to watch every coastal sunset, hoping to see the green flash. My hope shriveled as the years passed, and sunsets, even the most showy, always ended without a hint of green. In time, I quit looking for the extraordinary and became content to view a sun that set in the usual shades of yellow and red.

The green flash was all but forgotten when my husband and I took our six-year-old grandson camping in the summer of 1998. We pitched our tent near the beach at Cape Disappointment State Park on the Washington coast. Our first day there was perfect, warm, and sunny, calling for a twilight walk beside the waves.

As we headed down the sandy path leading from campground to beach, the sun lowered on the horizon. A ball of flame, I half expected to hear it sizzle as it sank into the cool green Pacific. Hurrying toward the beach I glanced between the log-strewn path and the glorious setting sun. I couldn't believe how rapidly the huge red ball was dropping. I wanted to stand and watch it, but the sandy lane was narrow and too busy for loitering.

Stepping onto the beach, I stood away from the trail to view the final moments of the sun's descent. My grandson beside me was as awestricken as I to see the variety of colors that sinking star displayed. Crimson, magenta, violet, and gold glowed before us in a matter of seconds. Then, with a shimmering flash of green and a sea-swallowed sun, the day was over.

It was real! The green flash existed, and I had seen it. Not that I was looking for it or even thinking about it. I was merely enjoying the beauty of the sea and sky, when the very thing I'd desired for so long appeared before my eyes.

As I marveled at the sun's parting glory, I realized this finding of joy when not seeking it had become a pattern in my life. Once I quit longing for the extraordinary and started finding pleasure in everyday things, I would, on rare occasion, be blessed with something as spectacular as a green-flash sunset.

My love for the beach and its beautiful sunsets continues. Who knows? Maybe one day I'll catch another phenomenal flash of green.

June Williams

"Catch of the Day"

If you surrender to the wind, you can ride it.

Toni Morrison

The sun rose over its watery hurdle, blazing down on a small boat swaying against sloshing waves. The craft bobbed up and down while two men maneuvered a leviathan-sized net through the water. A salty breeze stroked my face, leaving a thick, tacky glaze as I sipped the French roast, savoring its potent flavor. The coffee steamed down my throat, scouting a warm trail into my stomach. With staccato jerks a seagull's beak poked the water as he goose-stepped through the mushy sand searching for morsels to fill his belly. Like the gull, I too was searching for nourishment.

After months of writing I'd landed only a stringer of dis-appointments. Familiar surroundings cast no bait to tempt my hungry spirit—no subject lured my imagination. Convinced the mundane had suffocated my creative breath, I fled to the seaside, yearning to consume exotic delicacies and gorge my inspiration-starved appetite.

The fishermen stretched the net just off shore. As the

boat edged closer, one man jumped into a wave and pushed the dinghy the remaining distance. Once the boat was beached, a wispy youth, clad only in a pair of cut-offs, leaped ashore, hauling several buckets. Blond hair spiked up from a clean-shaven face, and two silver hoops dangled from his left earlobe. White sunscreen streaked beside squinted eyes that observed the confident motions of his partner's hands guiding the net inland.

The older man, his leathery skin seeping sweat, sported a thick gray-streaked ponytail at the nape of his neck. A T-shirt advising "Save Our Wildlife: Drive a Drunk Home" topped his swim trunks.

As if acting out his part in a long-running play, each performed his respective role, oblivious to the curiosity seekers congregating. Together they tugged until the net joined them ashore. The growing audience watched mesmerized as the net's contents spilled out to a chorus of oohs and aahs.

I'd assumed nothing of interest could be captured so close to shore but decided to go see what had initiated the rumblings. On the sand lay a conglomeration of the strangest creatures I'd ever seen. The fishermen began tossing some fish into buckets while returning others to sea. It appeared that the unusual creatures were freed while the ordinary ones were saved. Those in the buckets seemed too small for any retail value.

A woman wearing a wild floral shift spoke. "What's that over there?"

The older fisherman glanced to see which fish had been singled out. He scooped up a tiny, flopping fish. "A robin fish," he answered, raising it for inspection. "It got its name because the flippers on the side look like wings." He pitched the little fellow into the water. We watched as the miniature "wings" fluttered its escapee away.

"Look," called the boy, holding up a stingray, "looks like

we've caught this'n before." He laughed and pointed to a stinger laced straight-pin style in the ray's back and then said to the onlookers. "We remove the stinger so the ray won't hurt anybody. We don't kill any fish we don't need."

"Just what is your need?" I blurted out.

Without pausing, the man explained, "We collect food for a seabird sanctuary that nurses injured birds back to health. When a bird can survive on its own, it's freed. The boy and I feed the nursery. It takes a lot of fish for those babies. We work every day collecting the food—their very lives depend on it."

He set the fish-filled bucket on their boat, then grabbed another bucket and resumed the sorting.

I watched until the older man straightened. He gazed down the boundless coastline before he nodded at the boy. They walked the boat out to sea, jumped in and then rowed out farther, beginning the process once more.

As I witnessed their diligence, I envied their competence—soon realizing it was their diligence that created the competence. Like the gull, I'd feasted on tidbits from the sea that morning. They weren't the delicacies for which I'd longed, but rather the ones necessary to nourish my ailing writing. I'd waited too long for serendipity. I would return home to begin my daily seining and sorting, becoming a fisher capturing the words needed to give flight to my writings, fledglings of creativity.

Janice Alonso

The Shell

I watched my mother and two young daughters wading ankle-deep in the ocean on Lido Beach in Sarasota, Florida. Their long pants were rolled nearly to their knees, but still the bottoms were wet. We were searching for seashells to bring back home, but we weren't having much luck. My husband sprawled on the sand, his jacket rolled in a ball beneath his head. We were all trying to soak up the last few precious minutes of our vacation. Later that afternoon we would board a flight back to Chicago— back to freezing November temperatures, back to work and school. And unfortunately, back to reality.

This annual trip to Florida had become our Thanksgiving tradition. It began three years earlier as a celebration of my mother's recovery from surgery. A visit to the hospital for pneumonia had revealed a spot on her lung that was later diagnosed as malignant. The surgery to remove a section of her left lung had taken its toll on her physically, and on all of us emotionally. I'm an only child, so my mother and I have always shared a special bond. The thought of losing her was unimaginable to me.

As she began to regain her strength after the surgery, my mother suggested we all take a trip together. After such a difficult year, she wanted to build happy memories for my daughters, Sarah, eight, and Charlotte, six.

Though she had always been a sun-worshiper, that first year at the beach my mother spent much of the time in the shade or under the cover of a floppy straw hat. She wasn't taking any chances.

But she would do anything for her granddaughters, and when they begged their "Grammy" to swim with them she put on a bathing suit, despite the ugly scar that traversed her back. She played in the water and in the sand, even though she tired quickly. In the late afternoons, we all shared a frozen tropical drink, complete with a tiny paper umbrella.

That first year, shells were strewn on the beach like daisies in a field. There had been a storm the previous week, which seemed to have churned up the ocean and deposited all its treasures on the beach for us to choose from. We filled our pockets with dozens of shells and brought them home, where we displayed them in a huge glass jar. It sat on our mantle as a reminder of the special time we'd shared together on the beach.

But this year, our luck wasn't as good. We found fragments of shells, bits of sand dollars, and other uninteresting objects, but nothing worth saving. Our luck also matched our mood. Though we hadn't told Sarah and Charlotte, my mother's annual chest x-ray, taken just before we'd left, revealed a new spot on her lung. When we returned home, she would see her doctor to discuss what to do next.

I walked along the beach, not wanting to go home. Maybe if we stayed, we wouldn't need to return to reality. We'd bask in the warm sun, hear the calming rhythm of the waves, and enjoy our time together. I didn't want this vacation to end. I didn't want it to be our last.

I don't know what came over me, but I started talking to the ocean.

"Please, let everything be okay," I said. "Let us all come back here again next year. Together."

The waves continued to roll over the sand, licking my feet. I listened to the ocean. Was it listening to me?

"Send me a sign," I asked. "Send me a sign that everything will be all right."

I stood at the edge of the water, and in the distance saw my daughters walking hand in hand with my mother. I wanted to remember this moment, exactly as it was. It was one of those perfect moments you know you'll never be able to re-create.

I checked my watch and realized it was almost time to leave. In a few minutes, we would be brushing the sand from our feet, putting on our shoes and heading for the airport. Would we all be back again next year?

Just then, I noticed something in the water. With each wave, it moved closer to me, until it was almost at my feet. I took a step forward and picked up a conch shell as big as my hand. It was smooth, pink, and perfect. It was like no other shell we'd ever found. The ocean had given me a sign.

"Thank you, thank you," I whispered, imagining the shell at home on the mantle.

I took one more deep breath, filling my soul with the ocean's strength. And I knew everything would be okay. I knew it, because the ocean had told me so.

Ruth Spiro

The Family on the Beach

With the past, I have nothing to do; nor with the future. I live now.

Ralph Waldo Emerson

We're sitting in our car, my husband and I, parked near the beach, watching the sun slide below the wall of granite-gray clouds rising up from the horizon, out where the ocean ends. It's a beautiful evening. Here at sunset the shore is awash with muted pinks, pale yellows, and opalescent grays. Drained of daytime color, this seaside world of breaking waves and wet sand shimmers like the inside of an oyster shell.

It's chillier now than when we headed out to dinner earlier this evening. We didn't think then to bring along jackets or sweaters. So instead of walking off our desserts along this favorite stretch of beach, we decide to take in the scenery tonight from the comfort of two bucket seats, to hear the call of gulls through the car's open sun roof.

Nudging my husband's arm, I nod toward the young family ambling into view a few yards from the water's edge: mom, a dad, a little girl about five, and a boy who looks age three.

The dad, jacket collar turned up, stops to peer out at a big ship dredging sand about a half-mile offshore. The mom's gaze wanders from the setting sun to the seagulls overhead to the floppy cloth bag she's setting down in the sand.

From the bottom of this bag, the boy pulls out a plastic shovel and promptly sets to work: digging, scooping, and patting. His sister, all knees and elbows and Buster Brown bangs, sees this as her cue to perform for any beach-combers who care to watch what looks like the "Dance of the Purple Leggings."

The boy's intense focus and the girl's dramatic flair remind me of our two kids some seventeen years ago.

Today our daughter, a recent college grad, works at a nonprofit in the San Francisco Bay area. Our son, a specialist in the U.S. Army, sends e-mails from a base in Germany where he is stationed now after fifteen months in Iraq.

"Remember when Anne and Roman were that age?" I say to my husband.

"Barely," he answers softly.

"Where does the time go?" I wonder.

I can't take my eyes off this family. And for an instant, there is no such thing as time. There is only life, leaving its footprints on the beach. And at this moment, all that matters is these four people—with their zippered jackets and plastic shovels, their windblown hair and sand-filled sneakers. And this family is us: my husband, our daughter and son, and me. And we are them.

They won't know it, but I'll be there when they arrive back home—when the dad brushes the sticky sand from between his son's fingers and the mom pours a couple capfuls of Mr. Bubble into the warm, running water of the tub in the kids' bathroom. When the light from the lamp next to the family room sofa falls on the pages of tonight's bedtime story, I'll be there, too. In truth, I already am.

The family is about to leave the beach now. The dad scoops up the toy bag and reaches for the girl's hand as he turns to navigate the small incline that leads toward the cars. The little boy, still clutching his shovel, lifts both arms toward his mom. She picks him up. He wraps his legs around her waist, rests a cheek on her shoulder. Faces expressionless, they shuffle past our parked car.

This scene reminds me of Thornton Wilder's *Our Town*, where Emily, a character, asks in the play's final act, "Do any human beings ever realize life while they live it?" Wondering that very same thing, I feel impelled to pop up through the sunroof and call after these strangers, "Stop! Pay attention! Look, really look, at one another!" I want to tell them, "Tomorrow your little girl will study at a university hundreds of miles away! The day after that, your son will join the army. Before you know it, you'll have a condo in Sun City and five grandchildren! Stop, stay, look, really look."

Of course, I don't say any of this. Instead, my eyes follow them all as they head toward their car and home— toward days, nights, and years that will, I'm sure, pass far too quickly. But they can't possibly know that. Not now. Not next week or even next month. Maybe they'll have an inkling in another fifteen years or so, when one evening after dinner, this mom or dad or both drive to a nearby beach to watch the sun slide below a wall of clouds rising up from the horizon, out where the ocean ends.

There they'll notice a young family stopping near the water's edge. For a short while that holds within it echoes of eternity, they'll find they won't be able to take their eyes off that strangely familiar foursome. And without a word, they'll watch the long, end-of-day shadows stretching toward them across the sand—of a little boy and a dancing girl and a floppy bag of beach toys.

Sue Diaz

Flying with the Penguins

The day was slightly overcast—a perfect day for us to spend some time at the beach with Dominique. First we stood in the shallow water for a while to let the waves rush over our feet and splash us, much to her delight and sending her into fits of laughter and giggles.

We then sat side by side close to the water's edge to build sand castles and watched as the water came in to take them back into the ocean, leaving nothing but a smooth sandy surface as the pallet to begin yet another shovel and pail creation. We filled buckets of water and ran to share them with Mommy—well at least as much as was left after our bumpy journey through the hills of sand on our way back to the blanket and towels a few yards from shore. Dominique also searched for seashells while covering my legs, as well as her doll, with mounds of sand. It was a wonderful, calm, and enjoyable time in the middle of a summer vacation that I will forever remember.

Jackie and I began folding the towels and collecting the many scattered beach toys tossed here and there in the surrounding area. Dominique, however, wasn't quite ready to return to our condo for lunch. She had much bigger plans in store for me, as I soon found out.

"Oh, Momma, look at the penguins!" she exclaimed in that adorable squeal of an excited four-and-a-half-year-old.

"Can I touch them, please?" Her finger was pointed in the direction of a few wandering seagulls less than ten feet from where we stood. Her eyes were opened wide with excitement, but she stood there without moving until she was sure she had my full attention and approval.

Normally I would have taken a moment like this to teach her the difference between the two birds or would have at least corrected her choice of names to call these interesting creatures. But not this time. This time was different. Instead of leading—I followed. I let her teach *me* this time.

"Only if you can catch them!" I yelled as I grabbed my camera and threw the strap around my neck.

"Come on, Momma! Let's fly like the penguins!" With that she took off, her arms extended in a waving motion and little bare feet moving as quickly as she could manage through the warm sand.

I ran behind her half consumed with the joy of flying and the other half with an occasional pause to snap a photo of this beautiful moment. My heart was pounding and my eyes barely pushing back the tears as I watched her follow each bird in anticipation of being able to touch it if she was quick enough. As she came within a few feet of her goal, each seagull would take flight to escape her reach. Instead of being upset at the defeat, she would quickly turn and run in another direction as she spotted more skipping "penguins" waiting for her to play. Her "try, try again" attitude never wavered as she continued this game along the open beach. She hesitated only long enough to be certain I was still following her and to occasionally call out to me—"Wave your arms like this, Momma!" while demonstrating the motions.

This very special child, who barely walked a little more

than two years ago, was now "running" barefoot through the sand and "flying" like a champion. Much more than that—she has given me a gift I never would have dared to dream of receiving. I've read and heard the phrase "fly like an eagle" and thought I understood the meaning of the words. But now I've actually lived it in a way that few will ever know.

I've experienced the magic of flying with the penguins because my very special little girl took the time to show me how.

Sharon Rivers

As Good As It Gets:
A Seashore Snapshot

Once upon a time, my husband and I sat at a table at a Paris restaurant and watched, spellbound, as the flower-bedecked ceiling magically opened and doves flew overhead.

It was one of those dreamlike experiences, complete with magnificent food, violins, and romance in the City of Lights. We were young, carefree, and dazzled by the spectacular opulence, the food, the wine, and, of course, Paris itself.

As my late grandmother might have said, "What's not to like?"

What indeed?

So I have always clung to that dining experience as a milestone destined for the "as good as it gets" category.

But I've recently added another, so different as to be almost laughable—yet just as magical.

This time, dinner was not at a gilded restaurant with gold-rimmed china and tinkling crystal goblets. This time, it was on a modest deck at a beach house on Long Beach Island at the New Jersey seashore.

And this time, the cast of characters included our three daughters, our two sons-in-law, and seven very noisy, sunburned grandchildren.

It was not Paris, and it surely was not the Paris restaurant.

But it was just as magnificent a milestone.

Maybe it was the sight of the ocean from the deck of the rented house our daughters were sharing for one golden week at this glorious stage of their own lives.

Maybe it was the intoxicating smell of salt air mixed with charcoal from the well-used grill on this deck where Michael, the family gourmet-chef, was anointing fresh fish with his secret sauce.

Surely it was the spectacle of a fiery red sun setting over the bay and the sound of Danny's shrieks of delight as he chased his cousin Emily around the deck with the abandon of a four-year-old in love with life itself.

Definitely it was because I was holding tiny Baby Carly in my arms, protecting her from the stiff breeze and loving every moment my hands could touch her cloud-soft skin.

We sat on chairs that had seen better days, exhausted from the sun and surf, wrapped in jeans and sweatshirts, barely able to summon up the energy to move.

One of our daughters told a hilarious tale of a long-forgotten childhood escapade, and we laughed until our sides hurt.

Our "dinner service" was not the china and crystal of that Parisian restaurant, but the economy-brand supermarket paper plates and plastic forks that define summer at the beach.

And when Michael announced that his epic meal was ready, we ambled over to a picnic table to sample his artistry: the catch-of-the-day bluefish, the steaming corn, the grilled veggies that Michael insisted would nullify the calories yet to come from a decadent chocolate layer cake.

We all ate too much that night, and laughed more than

we had all summer, and fussed more than was prudent over little tykes with sand in their hair.

Chocolate icing coated Zay's hands, face, and sweatshirt. Hannah was staring at the moon, insisting that it was far too early for a young woman of ten to go to bed. And little Sam had fallen asleep on his grandfather's lap, still clinging to the shells he'd collected in his little yellow pail. Jonah was at perfect peace, asleep on the deck, clutching his "blanky."

There were no finger bowls, no French pastries, no doves that night.

But there was something far more precious.

There was a family at the beach, seizing one glorious day and night from the jaws of time, distance, and the frenzy of modern life.

And that made Paris pale by comparison.

Sally Friedman

"I hate to say it, but . . . do you think it is time to throw in the beach towel until next summer?"

Who Is Jack Canfield?

Jack Canfield is the cocreator and editor of the Chicken Soup for the Soul series, which *Time* magazine has called "the publishing phenomenon of the decade." The series now has 105 titles with over 100 million copies in print in forty-one languages. Jack is also the co-author of eight other bestselling books, including *The Success Principles: How to Get from Where You Are to Where You Want to Be, Dare to Win, The Aladdin Factor, You've Got to Read This Book,* and *The Power of Focus: How to Hit Your Business and Personal and Financial Targets with Absolute Certainty.*

Jack has recently developed a telephone coaching program and an online coaching program based on his most recent book *The Success Principles.* He also offers a seven-day Breakthrough to Success seminar every summer, which attracts 400 people from fifteen countries around the world.

Jack has conducted intensive personal and professional development seminars on the principles of success for over 900,000 people in twenty-one countries around the world. He has spoken to hundreds of thousands of others at numerous conferences and conventions and has been seen by millions of viewers on national television shows such as *The Today Show, Fox and Friends, Inside Edition, Hard Copy,* CNN's *Talk Back Live, 20/20, Eye to Eye,* the NBC *Nightly News,* and the CBS *Evening News.*

Jack is the recipient of many awards and honors, including three honorary doctorates and a Guinness World Records Certificate for having seven books from the Chicken Soup for the Soul series appearing on the *New York Times* bestseller list on May 24, 1998.

To write to Jack or for inquiries about Jack as a speaker, his coaching programs, or his seminars, use the following contact information:

The Canfield Companies
P.O. Box 30880 • Santa Barbara, CA 93130
phone: 805-563-2935 • fax: 805-563-2945
E-mail: info@jackcanfield.com or
visit his website at www.jackcanfield.com

Who Is Mark Victor Hansen?

In the area of human potential, no one is more respected than Mark Victor Hansen. For more than thirty years, Mark has focused solely on helping people from all walks of life reshape their personal vision of what's possible. His powerful messages of possibility, opportunity, and action have created powerful change in thousands of organizations and millions of individuals worldwide.

He is a sought-after keynote speaker, bestselling author, and marketing maven. Mark's credentials include a lifetime of entrepreneurial success and an extensive academic background. He is a prolific writer with many bestselling books, such as *The One-Minute Millionaire, Cracking the Millionaire Code, How to Make the Rest of Your Life the Best of Your Life, The Power of Focus, The Aladdin Factor*, and *Dare to Win*, in addition to the Chicken Soup for the Soul series. Mark has made a profound influence through his library of audios, videos, and articles in the areas of big thinking, sales achievement, wealth building, publishing success, and personal and professional development.

Mark is the founder of the MEGA Seminar Series. MEGA Book Marketing University and Building Your MEGA Speaking Empire are annual conferences where Mark coaches and teaches new and aspiring authors, speakers, and experts on building lucrative publishing and speaking careers. Other MEGA events include MEGA Info-Marketing and My MEGA Life.

As a philanthropist and humanitarian, Mark works tirelessly for organizations such as Habitat for Humanity, American Red Cross, March of Dimes, Childhelp USA, and many others. He is the recipient of numerous awards that honor his entrepreneurial spirit, philanthropic heart, and business acumen. He is a lifetime member of the Horatio Alger Association of Distinguished Americans, an organization that honored Mark with the prestigious Horatio Alger Award for his extraordinary life achievements.

Mark Victor Hansen is an enthusiastic crusader of what's possible and is driven to make the world a better place.

Mark Victor Hansen & Associates, Inc.
P.O. Box 7665 • Newport Beach, CA 92658
phone: 949-764-2640 • fax: 949-722-6912
www.markvictorhansen.com

Who Is Patty Aubery?

As the president of Chicken Soup for the Soul Enterprises and a #1 *New York Times* bestselling coauthor, Patty Aubery knows what it's like to juggle work, family, and social obligations—along with the responsibility of developing and marketing the more than 80 million *Chicken Soup* books and licensed goods worldwide.

She knows because she's been with Jack Canfield's organization since the early days—before *Chicken Soup* took the country by storm. Jack was still telling these heartwarming stories then, in his training programs, workshops, and keynote presentations, and it was Patty who directed the labor of love that went into compiling and editing the original 101 *Chicken Soup* stories. Later, she supported the daunting marketing effort and steadfast optimism required to bring it to millions of readers worldwide.

Today, Patty is the mother of two active boys—J. T. and Chandler—exemplifying that special combination of commitment, organization, and life balance all working women want to have. She's been known to finish at the gym by 6:00 AM, guest-host a radio show at 6:30, catch a flight by 9:00 to close a deal—and be back in time for soccer with the kids. But perhaps the most notable accolade for this special working woman is the admiration and love her friends, family, staff, and peers hold for her.

Of her part in the *Chicken Soup* family, Patty says, "I'm always encouraged, amazed, and humbled by the storytellers I meet when working on any *Chicken Soup* book, but by far the most poignant have been those stories of women in the working world, overcoming incredible odds and—in the face of all challenges—excelling as only women could do."

Patty is also the coauthor of several other bestselling titles: *Chicken Soup for the Christian Soul, Christian Family Soul,* and *Christian Woman's Soul, Chicken Soup for the Expectant Mother's Soul, Chicken Soup for the Sister's Soul,* and *Chicken Soup for the Surviving Soul.*

She is married to a successful international entrepreneur, Jeff Aubery, and together with J. T. and Chandler, they make their home in Santa Barbara, California. Patty can be reached at:

Self-Esteem Seminars
P.O. Box 30880
Santa Barbara, CA 93130
Phone: 805-563-2935
Fax: 805-563-2945

Who Is Peter Vegso?

Peter Vegso arrived in South Florida from Canada and founded the publishing company Health Communications, Inc., in 1976. HCI's first *New York Times* bestseller, *Adult Children of Alcoholics* (Woititz), appeared on the list in 1985 and has been followed by dozens more self-help and inspirational titles, including *Healing the Shame That Binds You* (Bradshaw), *A Child Called It* and *The Lost Boy* (Pelzer), and many titles in the Chicken Soup for the Soul series. Recognized twice by *Publishers Weekly* as the #1 Self-Help Publisher, HCI is guided in its publishing program by its mission statement, "Making a difference in the lives of our readers and the people they come in contact with."

Peter's other business interests include a professional publishing and conference company that provides training, licensing, and certification for members of the mental health community, a custom design and architectural elements manufacturer, and real estate development.

Peter enjoys his 140-acre farm in Ocala, Florida, where he continues to expand his successful thoroughbred breeding and training facility. Daily operations are handled by the hardest-working manager in the world, Chuck Patton, who shares Peter's intention to not only win the Kentucky Derby but also the Triple Crown before their spirits leave this planet.

Peter Vegso
Health Communications, Inc.
3201 SW 15th Street
Deerfield Beach, FL 33442
phone: 954-360-0909 • fax: 954-360-0034
website: www.hcibooks.com

Contributors

Elena Aitken is a freelance writer with her own copywriting business, Ink Blot Communications, in Calgary, Alberta. She keeps busy parenting her four-year-old boy/girl twins, volunteering in the community, and writing when she finds the time. You can contact Elena at leenie twins@shaw.ca or on her new website at www.inkblotcommunications.ca, which is coming soon!

Janice Alonso enjoys being with her family, inspirational writing, and traveling. Her work has appeared in *Grit, Lutheran Digest, Standard, Palo Alto Review,* and *Chicken Soup for the Christian Soul II.* Please visit her at www.janicealonso.com and leave her a message.

Paula F. Blevins and her husband, David, live in southern Ohio with three wonderful kids and their pets. She is the author of the *For Hymn* mystery series and a variety of Chicken Soup stories, and she enjoys writing for children as well as adults. Contact Paula through her website at www.paulafblevins.com.

Arthur Bowler, a U.S./Swiss citizen and graduate of Harvard Divinity School, is a writer and speaker in English and German. His work has appeared in several bestselling anthologies and in bestselling books in Switzerland. Look for his book, *A Prayer and a Swear.* Visit his website at www.arthurbowler.ch.

Julie Callas is a homemaker and mother of three inspiring children. She is a freelance poet and magazine writer who enjoys the Bible, the beach, and writing. She plans on publishing her first volume of poetry in the next year. Please e-mail her at thecallas@msn.com.

Anne Carter, a native New Yorker and freelance writer, dedicates this story to her two grandsons, Daniel and Dylan Delacruz, in memory of their beloved mother, Donna. May her amazing spirit always be with you. Anne's inspirational stories have appeared in major publications. Contact anne at carteracdc@webtv.net.

Emily Parke Chase writes for teens on relationship issues. Her first book was *Why Say No When My Hormones Say Go?* which was followed by *You, Me, and WHO? 5-Minute Devotionals for You and Your Date.* She speaks hundreds of times each year in schools and conferences on these topics.

JoAnn Clark was the founding editor and writer for her church newsletter.

Sally Clark and her husband live in the Texas Hill Country, but they love retreating to the sea. Sally has published humor, greeting cards, children's stories, and award-winning poetry, most recently in the 2007 *Texas Poetry Calendar* and *Relief: A Quarterly Christian Expression Journal.* E-mail her at auslande@ktc.com.

Lisa Ricard Claro enjoys writing personal essays, women's and children's fiction, and short stories in every genre. She has recently completed her first women's fiction novel. In addition to writing, Lisa's loves include her husband, their three children, reading, and beaches everywhere. Please e-mail her at lisaclaro@bellsouth.net.

Helen Colella is a freelance writer from Colorado. Her work includes educational materials, articles, and stories for adults and children. She operates AssitWrite as a consultant for self-publishers and writing coaches. E-mail her at helencolella@comcast.net.

Margaret P. Cunningham lives on Alabama's beautiful Gulf Coast with her husband, Tom. She enjoys reading, writing, and "beaching it" with family and friends. Her stories have appeared in magazines and anthologies, including several Chicken Soup for the Soul books. She is currently working on a novel. Please e-mail her at peggymob@aol.com.

Susan Allsbrook Darke has been in human resources management for more than thirty years. Currently living in northern Virginia, Susan and her husband plan to relocate to the Outer Banks in North Carolina in the near future. Susan enjoys reading, singing, dancing, writing, and spending time with family. E-mail her at sdarke@cox.net.

Bonnie Walsh Davidson, M.Ed., of Marion, Massachussetts, is the author of *Breast Friends.* Davidson has turned her breast cancer experience into an avocation, publishing numerous pieces on breast cancer in several national magazines as well as *Chicken Soup for Every Mom's Soul* (March 2005) and *Chicken Soup for the Sister's Soul* (October 2006). Her husband, Paul, encouraged her to spread her wings with a website, PinkRibbon.com, in the hopes of assisting other women diagnosed with breast cancer. Davidson is a mother of three and a full-time real estate associate for Jack Conway & Company, Inc., in Mattapoisett, Massachussets, and chairperson of the Relay for Life in her community.

Sue Diaz is an essayist, author, and writing teacher whose work has appeared in numerous regional and national publications, including *Newsweek, Family Circle, Christian Science Monitor, Woman's Day,* and *Reader's Digest.* She is also a frequent on-air essayist on National Public Radio. She can be reached via her website: www.suediaz.com.

Judy DiGregorio, a freelance writer from Oak Ridge, Tennessee, has published more than one hundred humorous poems and essays, including columns in the *Writer* and the *Army-Navy Times*. She was recently nominated by the Tennessee Arts Commission to their online registry (www.SouthernArtistry.com) as an outstanding southern writer.

Avis Drucker retired to Cape Cod with husband Al as "washashores" in 2001. Her memoirs and poetry have appeared in *Chicken Soup for the Soul Life Lessons for Women; Chicken Soup for the Shopper's Soul; World of Water, World of Sand* anthology; *The Philosophical Mother; The Aurorean; Primetime;* and in syndication with King Features Syndicate. She has two daughers, Leslie and Vicki.

Stefanie Durham is a freelance writer living in Florida with her husband and three amazing daughters. She captured a love for writing while attending East Tennessee State University and is currently working on her first novel. She can be reached by e-mail at stefaniedurham@comcast.net.

Karen Falk grew up on Long Island in New York. She received her degrees from SUNY Cobleskill, SUNY Oneonta, and CUNY Queens College. She is married and lives in Las Vegas. She is currently teaching third grade. This piece was written to model the writing process for her students. Karen vacations at any beach. She has wonderful memories of her family growing up at the beach club.

Carolyn Mott Ford lives near the ocean and enjoys walking along the beach. She writes poetry, essays, and stories, as well as early learners for children, and her work has been published in general, juvenile, and literary magazines, as well as anthologies.

Sally Friedman spent her summers growing up at the New Jersey seashore, where her mother taught her to love the ocean. She has transmitted that legacy to her own children and grandchldren. A longtime freelance writer, Sally has shared many of her reflections with readers of the Chicken Soup for the Soul series. E-mail her at pinegander@aol.com.

Paula Gunter-Best received her bachelor of arts with high honors from Eckerd College. Her hobbies include showing and breeding rabbits. She combines her love for children and for rabbits into a ministry providing practical messages of pet ownership with messages of divine love and acceptance for all God's beings.

Pamela Hackett Hobson (Peggy's daughter!) is the author of two novels: *The Bronxville Book Club* and *The Silent Auction*. Pam's debut novel,

The Bronxville Book Club, was featured in the *New York Times.* To learn more about the author and her writing projects, visit www. pamelahobson.com or send an e-mail to author@pamelahobson.com.

Patrick Hardin is a freelance cartoonist whose work appears in a variety of books and periodicals. He may be reached by phone at 810-234-7452.

Roberta Beach Jacobson considers herself a free spirit. At age twenty-one, she left Chicagoland to explore Europe. After more than two decades of wandering, she settled on the Greek island of Karpathos, where she spins words and feeds cats. Her website can be found at http://www.travelwriters.com/Roberta.

Karen R. Kilby resides in Kingwood, Texas, with her husband, David. She is a certified personality trainer with CLASServices, Inc., and a speaker for Stonecroft Ministries. Karen has had several short stories published and can be reached at krkilby@kingwoodcable.net.

Betty King is an author of three books, a freelance writer, and a lifestyle and devotional newspaper columnist and speaker who lives with the disease multiple sclerosis. Visit her website at www.betty king.net or e-mail her at baking2@charter.net.

Dolores Kozielski is a certified Feng Shui practitioner in New Jersey and Pennsylvania. She is an author and award-winning poet, published with major publishing houses including HarperCollins. Dolores is a contributor to *Chicken Soup for the Soul Healthy Living/Stress* and *Chicken Soup for the Soul Sister's Soul 2.* She may be reached at www. FengShuiWrite.com.

Jaye Lewis is an award-winning writer who, at age sixty, finds the trials of life, and its lessons, the best way to find out who you are. You can read more of Jaye's inspirational stories on her website at www.entertainingangels.org or e-mail Jaye at jayelewis@comcast.net.

Heather Cook Lindsay received her bachelor's from Mount Holyoke College and her master's from Harvard University. Heather is writing a memoir about her highly unusual life. She grew up in an oxygen tent, was disabled by thirty, and can usually be found writing or laughing with her husband. E-mail her at hclindsay@aol.com.

Andrea MacEachern currently resides in St. John's, Newfoundland, where she works from home as a freelance writer and volunteers with a local cable station as a camera person. She enjoys photography, swimming, and walking.

Audrey D. Mark is an award-winning writer and graduate of

Northwestern University. Her humorous columns appear in the *Raleigh News & Observer* and other publications. She has three great kids and an adoring husband, who thinks that even her grocery lists are cleverly written. Please e-mail her at Audrey@AudreyDMark.com.

Janet Matthews is a writer, editor, professional speaker, and coauthor of the bestselling *Chicken Soup for the Canadian Soul*. She has a new book entitled *The Navy's Baby*, for which she is currently seeking a publisher, and she is working on another book entitled *Discovering Your Spiritual Purpose*. To learn more about Janet or contact her, go to www.janet matthews.ca, or call 905-726-8000, or e-mail janet@canadiansoul.com.

Patrick McDonnell is a teacher living in Gilbert, Arizona. He received his M.Ed. from Nothern Arizona University and his undergraduate from St. John's (New York). He lives with his wife, Trish, and son, Thomas. He is also a high school football official. He can be reached at NYC2AZ@aol.com.

Sharon Melnicer is a writer, artist, and teacher in Winnipeg, Manitoba. She frequently broadcasts the "Slice of Life" pieces that she pens on CBC radio. A retired high-school English teacher, she continues to teach life-story writing to adults and is a recognized artist who shows and sells throughout North America.

George H. Moffett lives a short distance from the beach. His essays have appeared in newspapers and *Chicken Soup for the Recovering Soul Daily Inspirations*. George has been a surfer, U.S. Marine, municipal councilman, active church member, and now in his seventies is a writer. E-mail George at geomoffett@yahoo.com.

Dee Montalbano is a teacher, a teacher of teachers, a communication consultant, and a writer. She is mom to two grown daughters and grandma to three great kids. When she's not hiking, she cooks great soups, enjoys music and film, and spends as much time as possible in Tuscany. You can reach her at dmdblk@yahoo.com.

Amy Ammons Mullis lives with her husband and two teenaged sons in South Carolina in a town the size of a starlet's bikini. She works as a church secretary, but is retired from taking family vacations. Her muses are a pile of wet towels and a sand-filled swimsuit.

Linda O'Connell, an early childhood educator for thirty years, leaves St. Louis each June and heads to the beach with her husband. She also enjoys camping. Water and the great outdoors inspire her to write. She has been published in numerous anthologies, literary journals, and newspapers. Contact her at billin7@juno.com.

Colette O'Connor is a beach-based travel and lifestyle writer who is either working hard or hardly working around the Monterey Bay, California, area. When working hard she is editor-in-chief of *Flying Adventures*, a travel and lifestyle magazine for aviators. Her features, interviews, and essays have appeared in newspapers from the *Los Angeles Times* to the *Washington Post*, in magazines from *France* to *World Traveling*, and in the nonfiction travel anthologies *Travelers' Tales*, Paris edition (1997), *Sand in My Bra & Other Misadventures: Funny Women Write from the Road* (2003), and *Best Women's Travel Writing* (2006). She loves receiving e-mail at chezcolette@cruzio.com.

Maryann Pasqualone is retired from real estate and serves on the board of the Garden State chapter of the Myasthenia Gravis Foundation. Maryann lives by the Jersey Shore and organizes a fundraiser on the boardwalk each September for myasthenia gravis. Please e-mail her at mair11@aol.com.

Diane Payne teaches creative writing at the University of Arkansas–Monticello. She is the author of the novel *Burning Tulips*. Every summer, Diane and her daughter Ania visit Lake Michigan.

Stephanie Piro lives in New Hampshire (not too far from the beach!) with her husband, daughter, and three cats. She is one of King Features' team of women cartoonists known as the Six Chix (she is the Saturday chick!). Her single panel, "Fair Game," appears in newspapers and on her website: www.stephaniepiro.com. Her new book, *My Cat Loves Me Naked*, is available at bookstores everywhere. She also designs gift items for her company Strip T's.

Helen Kay Polaski is a freelance writer and book editor. Her work has appeared in various newspapers, books, and newsletters.

Sharon "Kaye" Rivers resides with her loving partner, Jackie, and their beautiful daughter, Dominique, in a small town in New Jersey. She's also the mother of two older children, Christopher and Misti, who are both living away in different states but always remain close to her heart. "To be given this chance to tell a story that's so dear to me is truly very exciting. Having experienced those precious moments on the beach through our daughter's eyes is one story I'm proud to share with everyone who chances to read it." Please e-mail her at SKaye05@aol.com.

Sallie A. Rodman is a California native and loves the beach any time of the year. She attended Cal State Long Beach and loves writing inspirational stories. Her work has appeared in numerous *Chicken*

Soup anthologies, various magazines, and the *Orange County Register.* Reach her at sa.rodman@verizon.net.

Linda W. Rooks is the author of *Broken Heart on Hold, Surviving Separation* (Cook, 2006) and has been published in several national magazines, including *Focus on the Family, HomeLife,* and *Tapestry.* She is listed in Who's Who and lives with her husband in Florida.

Kelly Salasin is a three-time contributor to the Chicken Soup for the Soul series. Her work, "The Ring," is in *Celebrating Mothers and Daughters,* and "The Circle of Life" is in *Chicken Soup to Inspire a Woman's Soul.* Kelly grew up on the Atlantic coast and writes from her current home in Vermont.

Harriet May Savitz is the award-winning author of twenty-four books, including *Run, Don't Walk,* an ABC Afterschool Special produced by Henry Winkler. Her new novel *Sidney! Sidney! Sidney!* and reissued books by *AuthorsGuild/iUniverse* can be found at www.iUniverse.com and www.harrietmaysavitz.com, or contact her at hmaysavitz @aol.com or at Essay Books at www.authorhouse.com.

Tracey Sherman received her bachelor's with teaching certification from Angelo State University in 1986. She has traveled the world with her husband, a career military officer, and has raised three wonderful children. She actively pursues her dream of writing for children and young adults. She can be reached at ShermanTL@aol.com.

Lee Silber is the award-winning author of eleven books and an avid surfer. In 1987 Lee and his brothers turned their passion for surfing into a successful business when they founded Waves & Wheels Surfcenters, Inc. The Silber family live in a beach house steps from the sand in San Diego, California. To learn more about Lee and read his beach blog, go to www.creativelee.com.

Marsha Brickhouse Smith attended the College of the Albemarle. She worked with a national television network for over twenty years before retiring to coastal North Carolina. She has been published by Blue Mountain Arts, *Christian Life* magazine, and local newspapers. She enjoys writing poetry and spending time with her grandchildren. She plans to write a women's devotional book.

Pamela Gayle Smith lives in Mount Vernon, Indiana. She has been married to John for thirty-seven years and has three daughters, Shannon, Jennifer, and Misti. She has eight grandchildren, Nicholas, Tara, Austin, Seth, Averie, Johnathan, Brandon, and Zachery. She enjoys traveling and meeting new people. She can be e-mailed at IndianaRhymer@aol.com.

Ruth Spiro lives in Illinois with her husband and two daughters, who provide endless inspiration for her writing. Her articles and essays have appeared in *Child, Woman's World,* and *Chicago Parent.* She is also the author of a children's book, *The Bubble Gum Artist.* She can be reached at ruth@ruthspiro.com.

Joyce Stark lives in northeast Scotland and has recently retired from local government. She is currently working on a book covering her travels in small-town/big-city USA and a book to teach Spanish to very young children. Her main hobby is socializing with people. E-mail her at joric.stark@virgin.net.

Jean Stewart is an award-winning California writer and editor, married for forty-six years, mother of twin daughters, grandmother of an incredible two, all of whom are fanatic beach lovers. Her stories can be found in *Chicken Soup* books for *Father-Daughter, Horse Lover II,* and *Dieter's Souls,* and other anthologies. She is also a travel writer and working on a parenting book.

Craig A. Strickland's family beach is "T-Street," in San Clemente, California. Craig A. Strickland has seen the publication of many short stories in both magazines and anthologies, plus (so far) two nationally distributed books. For more information, visit CraigStrickland.net.

B. J. Taylor spends time at the water's edge often. It is there that she appreciates the vastness of life. She is an award-winning author whose work has appeared in *Guideposts,* many Chicken Soup books, and numerous magazines and newspapers. She has a wonderful new husband, four children, and two adorable grandsons. You can reach B. J. through her website at www.clik.to/bjtaylor.

Karen Theis. Wife, mother, daughter, sister, and friend. A seven-year breast cancer survivor. Contributing author in the book *Chicken Soup for the Breast Cancer Survivor's Soul.* My stories are my own true experiences, and they are written from my heart.

Bernetta Thorne-Williams was born and raised in Washington, D.C. She received a bachelor's in criminal justice and a bachelor's in English from Wesleyan College. Bernetta currently resides in North Carolina with her husband and two sons. She was a contibuting author to *Chicken Soup for the African American Woman's Soul.* E-mail her at BernettaThorneWilliams@yahoo.com.

Terri Tiffany has a bachelor's in psychology and has counseled adults for almost twenty years. She co-owned a Christian bookstore before relocating to Florida. Terri enjoys meeting new people, spending time with her family, and traveling. She is currently writing an inspirational romance novel. Please e-mail her at talker445@yahoo.com.

Stefanie Wass lives in Hudson, Ohio, with her husband and two girls. A former elementary school teacher, Stefanie now enjoys being a stay-at-home mom, Sunday school teacher, and school volunteer. Her essays can be found in the archives at www.Heartwarmers.com.

June Williams lives in Brush Prairie, Washington, where she enjoys spending time with her children and grandchildren—and writing stories about them.

Ernie Witham writes the humor column "Ernie's World," which appears in the *Montecito* and *Santa Ynez Valley Journals* and is syndicated nationally. His column "Just For Fun" appears in each issue of *Chicken Soup Magazine*. His stories have also appeared in eight *Chicken Soup for the Soul* anthologies. He is on the faculty of the Santa Barbara Writers Conference and has led humor workshops in other parts of the country as well. Visit him at www.erniesworld.com.

Maggie Wolff Peterson has been a professional writer for twenty-five years. She lives in Virginia with her husband and dog.

Permissions

Family Cottage. Reprinted by permission of Sharon Melnicer. ©2006 Sharon Melnicer.

Not My Idea of the Hilton. Reprinted by permission of Bonnie Walsh Davidson. ©2006 Bonnie Walsh Davidson.

Caught on Video. Reprinted by permission of Andrea MacEachern. ©2006 Andrea MacEachern.

Frozen Dreams. Reprinted by permission of Diane Lynn Payne. ©2006 Diane Lynn Payne.

The Beach Club. Reprinted by permission of Karen Hahn Falk. ©2005 Karen Hahn Falk.

A Seacliff Serenade. Reprinted by permission of Colette O'Connor. ©2006 Colette O'Connor.

Sands of Time. Reprinted by permission of Emily Parke Chase. ©2006 Emily Parke Chase.

The Souvenir. Reprinted by permission of Karen Rae Kilby. ©2006 Karen Rae Kilby.

Summer Fun. Reprinted by permission of Julie A. Callas. ©2004 Julie A. Callas.

Daddy's Love. Reprinted by permission of Lisa Ricard Claro. ©2006 Lisa Ricard Claro.

Now and Then on the Beach. Reprinted by permission of Paula Gunter-Best. ©2006 Paula Gunter-Best.

Four Blocks Up. Reprinted by permission of Harriet May Savitz. ©2006 Harriet May Savitz.

Condo Without a View. Reprinted by permission of Judy DiGregorio. ©2001 Judy DiGregorio.

Dolphins. Reprinted by permission of Margaret Pearson Cunningham. ©2005 Margaret Pearson Cunningham.

The Ocean's Gift. Reprinted by permission of JoAnn Clark. ©1993 JoAnn Clark.

Turtle Dreams. Reprinted by permission of Judith M. Lewis. ©2004 Judith M. Lewis.